Stories and Essays from Genesis 1-11

JOHN M. JOHNSON

May these stories add
joy & insight to your
life & walk with Christ.

Blessings,

John M. Johnson

The Mirror

Stories and Essays from Genesis 1-11

JOHN M. JOHNSON

ILLUSTRATED BY FARID FADEL

Chinaberry House
P. O. Box 505
Anderson, Indiana 46015-0505
www.2Lights.com

Copyright © 2003
April 2003
All rights reserved.
For permission to reproduce any part
or form of the text, contact the publisher.

ISBN 0-9632180-8-5
Printed in the United States of America

DEDICATION

Maddie and Clem Dreger
and
Ann and Nathan Smith
who mentored us in the "how to's"
of missions,
who modeled for us a Christian marriage,
and who mirrored God's grace.

ENDORSEMENTS

*T*he oldest question in the world: how did all of this world come to be?

The oldest answer in the world: the imaginative creation of an unresting God expressing himself out of his very being. The meta-story of all time; the story of stories; the context for all our thinking, living, and being—contained in these eleven chapters of Genesis.

In *The Mirror* this meta-story, through the creative thoughtfulness of writer and artist, is unpacked again for our time, challenging us to see ourselves in this ancient tale of love, sin, and death, as old as humanity, as fresh as today: the story of God followers, staying in touch, falling out of grace, but never falling so far that God's love cannot reclaim.

Arthur Kelly
Coordinator for Communication and
Publishing for Church of God Ministries
Anderson, Indiana

*J*ohn Johnson has brought the creativity and mind of an artist to the reader as he looks deep into the beginning chapters of Genesis to find hope for the present day. Through story he retells the story of humanity's start in the created order of God. His vivid description of creation and the journey of the peoples of **the promise** engage the reader in wonder and awe. The *Book of Genesis* and *The Mirror* could be read side by side for teaching purposes in the family or in a study session with all ages engaging their own story.

Juanita Evan Leonard, Ph.D
Professor of Christian Mission
Anderson University School of Theology
Anderson, Indiana

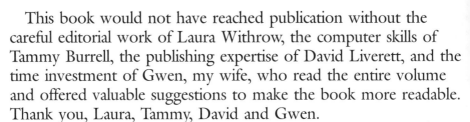

WITH APPRECIATION

This book would not have reached publication without the careful editorial work of Laura Withrow, the computer skills of Tammy Burrell, the publishing expertise of David Liverett, and the time investment of Gwen, my wife, who read the entire volume and offered valuable suggestions to make the book more readable. Thank you, Laura, Tammy, David and Gwen.

If, in any way, this small book of stories adds value and insight to you the reader, it is in large part due to the efforts of these four persons.

FOREWORD

*E*arly this morning, before sunshine broke through the darkness of night, 2000-pound bombs fell from the skies above Iraq and missiles rained upon Baghdad. Light brightened the sky, but it was not the sun's light; it was firelight. As morning dawned, the sounds of sleepy people waking to a new day were replaced by the sounds of war, the sounds of destruction, the sounds of fear. Rather than the smell of hot bread and cheese and strong coffee, the acrid smell of burning rubble, fuel oil and dust filled the air. On this first day of spring, the promise of new life is not so obvious in Iraq; it is not so hopeful, for the death toll mounts and the wailing and mourning has begun.

Having evacuated from Lebanon less than 24 hours ago, I write these words and wonder. How has it all come to this? What is it in our makeup as human beings that so compels us toward hatred and violence? What convinces us that the only possible response to another's hate and violence is more of the same? In this wonderful book of familiar and yet unfamiliar stories, John Johnson cracks open a window and lets a tiny shaft of light illumine some very disturbing answers to those questions. Yet it is in the midst of the ugly that we also see and hear and feel the resplendent majesty of our merciful and lovingly creative God who ushers in springtime even as humankind rains down destruction.

The Mirror is story within a Story. It is my story and it is your story. It is the story of how we came to be. And, it is the story of our faith, our striving through much unfaithfulness, to know the faithful God. A friend recently told me that he never reads fiction because "it just isn't true." "What makes something true?" I asked him. "Must all the facts be exact to some particular in-time reality for something to be true?" The stories you will read in this book are not true in the sense that they do not tell The Story the way we typically read it. But they are true in the deepest sense of the word for they speak to you and to me at the core of who we are, they tell our stories, and they tell the story that we are experiencing once again in that place where the Tigris and Euphrates rivers flow, the place where Scripture records that history began, the place where, even now, bombs fall.

The first eleven chapters of Genesis serve as the basis for John's stories. These chapters contain many familiar stories, but John retells them in unexpected ways and often from surprising perspectives. He raises many of the theological and biblical questions we've all asked at one time or another but he asks them in provocative ways that pose their own sets of questions. Sometimes John answers those questions directly. Sometimes his story suggests its own answer, interpreted by the individual reader. Sometimes he simply lets the questions hang in silence. But always, the horrible and lovely truth stretches the mind and moves the heart.

Generations before they were written, the Genesis stories were stories told around the fireplace and in community gathering places. They were told and retold and the voicing of them held their own mystery and power. In the same way, John's stories come alive when spoken out loud. The rhythms and rhymes dance more enthusiastically. The colorful words splash before the mind's eye with more vividness. The words full of richness and sound resonate the fibers of the soul. And once or twice, the truth spoken out loud will leave you speechless. Read these stories, these stand-alone and stand-together stories, out loud and,

THE MIRROR

as for generations long since past, they will also speak with mystery and power.

One of my personal favorites in *The Mirror* is entitled, "A Heart Attack, Who God?" This tells the story of God. It is the story of the Bible. It is the story of our times. It is the story being lived out in Iraq and in Heaven even as I write. It begins:

> God slumped on the rim of the world and wondered what things would have been like if Adam and Eve would have obeyed, if Cain would have listened, if revenge hadn't reared its ugly head, if innocence wouldn't have ceased to exist, if humankind wasn't so self-seeking and self-serving, if his marvelous creation hadn't been ravaged. Pain gripped the heart of God. God was having a heart attack.

If the story of the Bible is true, and I believe it is, then God is having a heart attack today. Yet pain and faithlessness, horror and ugliness do not tell the whole story.

> Amazing. God's massive coronary of the cross brought us righteousness. And our righteousness of being found in Christ brings healing to God's heart.

Don Deena Johnson
Fritzlar, Germany
March 20, 2003

TABLE OF CONTENTS

INTRODUCTION

*T*here it was. A mirror. Who in their right mind would place a mirror at the edge of a wilderness trail? It was not as if this trail were a busy, single-lane road through the mountains where you needed the mirror to be able to safely negotiate a hairpin turn. No, on the contrary, the mirror had been placed on a rather straight stretch of trail out in the middle of nowhere.

Perhaps it had been placed there for some sort of advertisement. But, on closer examination, there was nothing written on the mirror. There was no message about a hot shower, a cold drink, or a good bed, all of which anyone who made it this far on the trail would be craving just about now. But, no. Nothing. Just a mirror.

So what did the mirror do if it didn't advertise something? It reflected the truth. It reflected the truth about the surrounding nature. Green pines, gravelly dirt, yellow wildflowers, and the occasional chipmunk that would peer innocently into the mirror from a nearby boulder and then skitter away. And of course the mirror reflected the trail. Depending on where one stood one could see various parts of the trail.

One could easily see the beauty of nature in the mirror and the trail, but upon closer inspection, one could come to learn something about the God who had created the verdant meadow through which the trail meandered, by which the mirror had been placed. The Creator's extravagant use of color and texture, his clearly patterned order and precision, revealed a composition of unspeakable grandeur and harmony. All of this was clearly evident. God's fingerprints were everywhere. His signature was clearly evident. His character disclosed. His plan and purpose made manifest. That God used the mirror to reveal himself to passersby was obvious, obvious, that is, to those who took the time to look deeply within the mirror.

The mirror also reflected the truth about the occasional hiker or hunter who trekked by on this particular stretch of the trail. Often it was a scratchy beard, disheveled hair, dirty clothes, and tired eyes that were reflected in the face of the mirror.

One or two hunters, it seems, had taken pot shots at the mirror. Perhaps at a distance these hunters had seen some movement and fired, only to discover that what they had bagged was the mirror. Maybe these hunters had caught a glimpse of their own reflections and, not liking what they had seen, fired at point blank range. Apparently one hiker had taken out his camping knife and tried to deface the mirror for the same reason. What they hoped to do was to destroy the mirror. If they were able to destroy the mirror then they would be able to continue their hunt or journey shielded from the knowledge of what they were really like. Long ago someone once wrote, "Seeing their reflection in a mirror they promptly walked away and forgot what they looked like." In this case, however, these hunters and hikers sought to destroy the mirror so they would never be drawn back to see a true reflection of themselves, the world around them, or the Creator God.

But this mirror had been set beside the trail by God. The mirror had an enduring, everlasting quality about it. It would stand the test of time. What could a few hunters and hikers along the wilderness trail possibly do to it?

The first eleven chapters of Genesis are very much like the mirror mentioned above. The stories within these chapters have not been given to us as curiosity pieces, something we play with for a time and then discard when we grow weary of them. No! Rightly understood, these stories mirror truth. When we rightly look into these stories we are forced to see nature, God, and ourselves in a true way. Of course we can take pot shots at these stories. People often do. "These stories prove God's Word is unreliable. Whoever heard of a talking snake?" "Legends!" "I believed those stories when I was a child, but come on, give me a break. They are just stories. They are not true. They are just the stuff of fancy."

Genesis one through eleven is made up of stories. Yes, that is correct. But again, they are truthful stories. They are not scientifically authentic textbook descriptions. Nor are they eyewitness accounts of the first moments of creation or man's first brush with the "law."

These stories tell us what nature is. It is God-created. It is well ordered. It is good. It is under humanity's dominion. It is for humanity's good. It is God's generous provision.

These stories also tell us that we were created to be a people formed for a holy relationship with God and a caring, nurturing, revitalizing relationship with each other. Sadly these stories reveal our true condition: sinful, pride-filled, self-centered, and rebellious.

Not only do these stories reveal what nature is, the persons we were created to be and what we have become, but they also tell us who God is. He is the loving Creator, caring Father, holy Lord, righteous Judge, and redeeming Savior. All of that is what I mean when I say that these stories are "true."

In order to get the most out of these stories it would be most helpful if the text or texts mentioned below each title would be read first. Now, of course, that is not necessary. Hopefully the message of the story will shine through. Nonetheless, by reading the biblical account first you will be able to catch some of the details within the story that will be examined in the story or essay that follows. If nothing else, you will be reminded of the flow and flavor of the Genesis account. Remember, the true reflections of nature, yourself, and God are found in the biblical stories of Genesis 1-11. The reflective properties of stories and essays in this collection are but tarnished brass when compared to the crystal clear mirror of God's Word.

These short stories and essays that follow are fanciful, to be sure. Some might even say that they are the product of an imagination gone awry. What I have sought to do in this collection is to let the biblical stories speak afresh, to let the reflective qualities of the mirror shine through. To the extent that I have failed and clouded the mirror, so to speak, I ask for your mercy. To the extent that I have succeeded, I give praise to God, my Creator, my Redeemer and Sustainer.

John M. Johnson
Beirut, Lebanon
December 2002

Formed and Filled Up

Genesis 1

God created. He spoke. He fashioned. He called forth. In a place that was formless and void God did something truly marvelous. On the first three days of creation God envisioned and called into being a glorious place of habitation. Yet, there was not habitation. That was what God set about doing on the three succeeding days, filling up the emptiness. And God did all things so very well.

When God rolled up his sleeves and got down to the serious business of filling up this vast created emptiness of water, sky and land, he did so according to a fantastic plan. The waters teemed with life, the tiniest plankton to the biggest whale and an amazing array of life in between. The skies burst forth with winged movement, fast furious hummingbird-like movement and graceful, floating, gliding-on-the-wind currents, eagle-like movement. And the land exploded with cud-chewers, other-chewers, gazelle and bovines, panthers and pumas.

And God determined that each creature should be created "according to its kind." When God began his creative process he looked down at his pre-planned blueprints and did everything according to kind. However, when God created man he looked and looked for a suitable model, a form. He found nothing. He turned his workroom upside down looking for his sketches of what man would look like. In his search he glanced in a mirror and the idea exploded on him with such delight it took his breath away. Birds, fish, and animals made according to their kind. Man made according to the image of God himself.

And to this humanity, patterned after God's image, God bestowed the gift of sovereignty over all that he had previously created. What was once formless and void was now tangible. And what was empty was now filled. Over all that God had made he pronounced a blessing. "This is very good!"

The Gala Premiere

Genesis 1

The movie was in the can. Production had been completed. It was a documentary. God's first work entitled, "Creation." It was to go on to become one of God's finest movies. In fact, in all of recorded history God's first work, "Creation," and its sequel, "Redemption," were stories of very rare quality indeed. But production had not as yet begun on the movie "Redemption." Oh, to be sure, it was already in the mind of the writer, producer, and director – all who just happened to be God.

The premiere showing of "Creation" was set for the eighth day at sunset. All the big names were to be present: Duckbill Platypus, California Sea Lion, Hammerhead Shark, Reticulated Giraffe…the list went on and on. In fact, every creature that God had created and who, thereby, appeared in the documentary was given an invitation to the gala event. And humankind, man and woman, were invited, too. They, in fact, were God's honored guests. When they appeared at the premiere a hush went over the gathered assembly. To none of his creation did God bestow such honor. God himself was standing at the head of the vast crowd waiting to be the first to greet man and woman as they arrived. And then God himself escorted them to their specially assigned seats. Only when man and woman were in their places did the first showing begin.

And what a show! The musical score was marvelous. It matched the film exactly. Lilting flutes, filtering violins, crashing cymbals, stirring timpani, golden brass. Goose bumps appeared not only on the gaggle of fowl in the balcony; everyone experienced them. Spines tingled. Hearts pounded. Gasps of breath could be heard throughout the auditorium as God created species after species, family after family. At times the assembly burst into laughter, like when the skunk rubbed up

19

against a white lamb whose paint was still wet. And applause? Oh, there was applause. The roof nearly came off the place when God flung the stars into space. Oohs and ahhs were heard across the theater as in high-speed projection God took a seed, planted and watered it, and in seconds it blossomed in glorious color.

Everyone was waiting for the creation of man. All in attendance were longing to see God's finest workmanship in living color. God's voice boomed through the speakers, which literally wrapped themselves around the room. "Let us make man in our own image!" What special effects! God was shown gazing into a mirroring mountain lake. God extended his hand into the water ever so slowly. Not a ripple was made in the water. And God scooped out that image so gently. In the blink of an eye man and woman stood beside God on the shore, God embracing his creatures. Lover and the beloved. The music swelled at just the right moment. The music said so well what all the created order knew in their hearts: "God, you've really outdone yourself this time!"

At the end of the film, instead of credits, these words scrolled across the screen:

"All creatures of our God and King
Lift up your voice and with us sing,
Alleluia! Alleluia!"

It was an amazing response. There has never been anything like it before or since. One would have expected a thundering of appreciation. But what thundered was the silence. Every creature bowed in reverence before his or her Creator. And the purest voice among them, a nightingale, sang acappela:

"Let all things their Creator bless
And worship Him in humbleness.
O praise Him! Alleluia!
Praise, praise the Father, praise the Son,
And praise the Spirit, Three in One!
O praise Him! O praise Him! Alleluia! Alleluia!
Alleluia!"

Confidence on Day Six

Genesis 1:24-31

God, the Creator with a well-trained eye for detail, was extremely confident on day six as he set about the task of calling humanity into existence. Previously he had spoken into being light and darkness, with all the shades, hues, and tints of dawn and dusk thrown in for good measure. Earth and sky had been formed at his command. The earth from its snow-capped Himalayan peaks to its deathly hot valleys. And the skies full of vast pressure systems and thermal currents and gentle breezes. God fashioned the land and the sea and all the places on land in between where water collects on its way to the sea: swampy marshlands, rushing rivers, lazy lakes and expectant wadis. God formed fish and fowl: whales and warblers, stingrays and sparrows, clown fish and condors. And land animals were not forgotten either. Horrifically huge, long-necked, naked-tailed, bushy-maned, blazingly fast. Everything imaginable, from these traits down to their extreme opposites, with a mind-boggling variety spanning the vast continuum.

Next God spoke man and woman into his perfect world. God's confidence was in full bloom. And in the midst of his confidence God did a tremendously risky thing. He assigned humankind with the responsibility and ability to care for his world. Man was to nurture this marvelous creation. Mankind was called to pilot the ship with the freedom to make all the mid-course corrections deemed necessary.

Was God out of his mind? Did he not know that man

would fall? Could he not imagine that his highly-valued creations would turn away? Did he not foresee that man would misinterpret dominion for exploitation? Did his confidence blind him to the nearness of the cliff of temptation and the shattering rocks of haughty self-proclaimed independence at the bottom of the chasm? Was God so confident that he forgot to look both ways before he crossed the road and was therefore blind-sided by man's runaway desire to rule?

No! This God with the well-trained eye for detail knew full well the damp, dark, dungeon-like depths into which man would soon descend. Still God was confident. "How," you ask, "in the midst of this sickening reality could God remain so confident?" Was God so dense? The confidence through which God viewed humanity must have been like bottle-thick glasses. His vision was distorted, right?

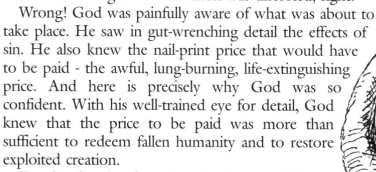

Wrong! God was painfully aware of what was about to take place. He saw in gut-wrenching detail the effects of sin. He also knew the nail-print price that would have to be paid - the awful, lung-burning, life-extinguishing price. And here is precisely why God was so confident. With his well-trained eye for detail, God knew that the price to be paid was more than sufficient to redeem fallen humanity and to restore exploited creation.

Yes! On day six of creation God was confident.

The Sabbath and the Seventh Inning Stretch

Genesis 2:1-4

*B*aseball gives us the famous seventh inning stretch. It's a time to give your backside a little relief from those hard, often backless, seats that you have had to pay top dollar for. The seventh inning, to those who, like my sister, dearly love attending a ball game (she hums "Take Me Out to the Ball Game" on dreary mid-February days), is the respite between what has gone on before and the real press toward the game's dramatic (hopefully) conclusion which occurs in the ninth inning, if the game doesn't go into extra innings. The seventh inning is the time where you stretch, go out for a soft drink and a bag of peanuts, make a quick pit stop, and return to your seat just as C-H-A-R-G-E! is flashing across the screen and your favorite batter is standing at the plate waiting until you take your seat before he steps into the batter's box. You know. The seventh inning. Not quite complete, the end in sight.

God apparently didn't have a seventh inning stretch from his task of calling forth light and darkness (thus forever making a distinction between day and night games), making a dome in the sky (not to be confused with the Skydome, or the King Dome, or even the Astrodome), dividing land and water (essential for base paths and rain delays), and creating fish, birds and animals (obviously to serve as mascots for our favorite teams like the Marlins, the Blue Jays and the Cubs). God also created humankind to play under the lights or in the dome, run the base paths, fret the rain delays, field the ball on grass, and wear the uniforms with the names of the mascots.

I'm so glad that the writer of Genesis didn't know the first thing about baseball when he wrote about the Sabbath (not to be confused

with a Sunday afternoon when baseball is often played).

It is amazing to me that of all the things God created, and he said all of his creation was "very good," it was the Sabbath that he blessed and made holy. Was God tired after all that he had done? Were his creative circuits on overload after extending himself beyond all limits to create a perfect world? No, I don't think that is what the text is saying at all.

God created a rest for mankind. A completeness. A wholeness. A holy wholeness where humankind can find peace and fulfillment. Yes indeed, there is a rest for the people of God.

There is a holy Sabbath. It is found in Christ. The seventh inning stretch isn't the Sabbath. Maybe death is the seventh inning stretch, the pause between what has gone on before here on earth and the final rush toward the consummation of all things in Christ.

Up From the Dust

Genesis 2:4-7

*O*ne of the first Arabic words we learned after arriving in Egypt was *torab*. The word simply means "dust." Truthfully, one of the questions we practiced in those early days of language study was "Why is there *torab* on the table?" My wife and I looked at each other incredulously. Were we really understanding this question correctly?

This is Cairo where the desert's dust daily mingles with man-made pollutants to make a cocktail that is hard to swallow, let alone breathe. Just down the Nile from our home were twenty-nine cement factories that hourly belch what must be tons of fine white powder into the air. If the wind was blowing our way, the dust ended up all over everything, not just on the table. You could clean a room, shut all the doors and windows tightly, go away and return a few minutes later and the tops of all your furniture looked like a petri dish gone crazy. In Cairo, where sunlight streams and headlights glow, dust descends and almost multiplies before your eyes, as if light were a key ingredient in the reproductive process of dust.

But why all this talk about dust? Well, it is because God created it, blessed it, and used it. God apparently was looking for a suitable construction material when he set about the task of creating man. We are not told that in some laboratory at the edge of creation God began testing various materials, discarding biodegradable plastic and ocean kelp because he happened on the by-product of dirt.

No. God took a most common material, the most readily available stuff, and formed something very similar to other aspects of his creation. But into the nostrils of this well-formed dust ball God breathed, into this up-from-the-dust-man God blew the breath of life. The common was filled with life and meaning. Man became a living being, "a completed soul," as a direct translation from the Hebrew text reads.

What's the point? The point is this. God can take the most common things in your world; things that you might like to discard, disregard, disown, and disassociate yourself with and use them. God can even take the dust and dirt of your life, fashion it, and then, by means of his Spirit, use it as personalized equipment to bring you closer to him and, in the process, bring glory to himself.

When the Chief Actor Spoke

Genesis 1, John 1, Colossians 1:16; Hebrews 1:1-3

There was no platform, no stage upon which the Chief Actor could perform. But that wasn't all. There was no backstage either. There was no sound system, no set, no props, no costumes, no curtains, no stage door, no orchestra pit, no lighting, no catwalks, no theater seats; in fact, there was no theater. Nothing! To be honest there was no set designer, no manager, no director, no prompter, no ticket sellers or ticket takers. There were no ushers with flashlights in hand that would lead well-dressed patrons of the arts to their seats. There were no patrons! There was no audience, no eager customers queued in long lines ready to see this performance – no one – not a person in sight, anywhere! Even if there were paying customers or even a few who managed to sneak in (and there were neither), there were no seats, numbered or unnumbered. There wasn't even the proverbial hook to pull the Chief Actor from view should the performance fail, and it surely seemed that from the very beginning it was destined to flop, destined to fail. Who would begin a production of this magnitude under such appalling conditions?

As the Chief Actor strode across the dense, black emptiness of space there was no drum roll, no applause, no stirring of anticipation … nothing! Under the Chief Actor's feet there was a roaring, surging, frothing ocean, an ocean straining with all its might to swallow or somehow subdue the Chief Actor. It wasn't an ocean of water but an ocean of chaos. But the Chief Actor gave the cacophonous sea not the slightest regard. The Spirit of the Actor was moving on, beckoning the Actor to begin the drama, to commence with the production, to let the show begin.

The Chief Actor spoke! It was no Shakespearian oration complete with exaggerated gestures, no, not at all. The Chief Actor spoke as one who was used to commanding vast armies. He spoke firmly, directly, powerfully. He spoke and it was clear he expected to be obeyed. There was no strain in his voice, no wavering or uncertainty. His word was sure and his voice carried across the face of the churning, tempestuous ocean of confusion.

At the sound of his voice startling changes began to occur. Light began to shine: good, generous, plentiful, life-giving light. Day and night were born. Sky, land, and sea were all fashioned out of the amazing imagination of the Chief Actor. No one was present but, if they had been privy to the creative genius of the Chief Actor, one might have thought the Chief Actor was improvising. However, on closer inspection, almost in hindsight, one would clearly have recognized the thrilling order of it all. It was obvious the Chief Actor was working from a script that the Chief Author had carefully and painstakingly crafted before the dawn of time.

Day, night, sky, land, and sea all were created in precise order. The earth produced lush, vast swaths of dense foliage and vegetation. It appeared in rapid succession, in the blink of the eye, from tiny tendrils of green to mammoth redwoods, and all manner of plant life in-between, all appearing, all bearing delightful fruit, all at the sound of the word spoken by the Chief Actor.

The velvety sky became a vast tablecloth of sorts. It was as if the Chief Actor put on an immense blindingly-white apron and appeared as a gourmet chef. He cradled the darkness of far-flung galaxies in his hand like an egg. With swift, deft movements he cracked the orb on the lip of a rocky precipice. Instantly the yoke of the sun and the white of the moon spilled forth, not into some mixing bowl-shaped valley but onto the tablecloth of the firmament. Where the egg white splattered stars and constellations appeared. It was not a mistake, the egg on the tablecloth. It was by design. Seasons and years all found their beginning in that moment. And it was all begun with the word.

The Chief Actor scanned the twinkling heavens above and the luxurious earth below with his steady gaze. It was as if he were searching for something on the far horizon, some movement out on the edge of where sky and earth meet. And he was not disappointed. In the sky small specks could be seen, insects perhaps. But it was not so. Soon the sky was covered with winged creatures of wondrous color, unimaginable design, and breath-taking variety. Some swooped and soared and others flitted and darted.

The earth was not left devoid of animal life. What started as a small cloud of dust out in the unidentifiable distance became uncountable herds of small, springing, fleet-footed creatures and slothful, seemingly over-weight, armor-plated mammals with every odd and fantastic creature spanning the spectrum between. And the creatures of the waterways were there as well: playful and fierce, translucent and transparent, bottom-dwelling and sky-flying. Whether in the air, on the land, or in the sea, all that huddled or hurried, meandered or mingled, wriggled or wrestled, plodded or paced, trotted or trounced, glided or grazed, sailed or stomped, migrated in herds or took to flight in solo air shows ... all were created by the Chief Actor, all came to life at the word.

The Chief Actor had erected a marvelous theater of sorts. All of creation was the stage, the props, the curtains, the backdrop upon which the Chief Actor called forth humans, beings like the Chief Actor Himself. These humans would manage the theater, so to speak. They were to rule over all, protect all, and steward all that the Chief Actor had called into existence.

The Chief Actor blessed his most perfect creation. All was created in the span of a few days and all was created with the word. What was that mighty, creative word? That word was "Jesus."

After the Chief Actor spoke the word "Jesus," he threw back his mighty head and celebrated. The word sounded throughout the universe like thunder, but not angry thunder. It was a riotous, celebrative, joyous Divine rumble that peeled like a newly minted bell. The Chief Actor could not have withheld his benediction even if he had tried. "All this is very good!" And the cosmos answered back in rapturous praise. "Amen!" they repeated and repeated again.

When the Co-Actors Spoke

Genesis 3 and I Peter 1:19-20

ll was glorious light and delightful perfection in the garden, the theater of God's own making. There was balance, harmony, and health. In the rich forests just enough light filtered through the massive branches for mosses, wildflowers, and small saplings to take root and grow. In forest meadows butterflies and bees danced from one colorful flower to another. The sun was warm and it dried the dew quickly in the meadow. The air was cool and clean. At indistinguishable intervals mountains broke through the forest ceiling stretching to the sky. The peaks were covered with a white mantle of snow. As the snow melted it filled the creeks and rivers of the garden so that there was an ample and eternally fresh supply of water, satisfying every resident of the garden, plant or animal. The water, at the decree of the Chief Actor, was ever in search of the lowest spot in which to settle. As a result the water trickled, gurgled, boiled, and literally raced to the seas.

Where the forest gave way to the seacoast was a dazzling sight to behold. At the coast the Chief Actor blended the lighter greens of the forest canopy with the various shades of black and the dark browns of the shadows, the dazzling white of the sand, and the multiple blues of the sea: aqua marine, emerald, turquoise, and indigo. It was as if the Chief Actor, in a passionate display of love for his creation, pulled out all the stops. Nearby, rushing over a rocky outcropping some sixty meters above, a river thundered over the edge and cascaded into a churning pool before finding its way to the sea.

The theater of the Chief Actor's design was marvelous beyond imagination. There was no smell of buttery popcorn in this theater. Instead the smells of the damp earthen forest floor, the salty sea, pungent and juicy ripening fruit, hibiscus and roses, pine, and lavender – all mixed together into a divinely inspired, mysterious potpourri. All those glorious smells and more!

Into this theater the Chief Actor placed his co-actors. Earlier it was said that the production of creation was destined to fail because the conditions prior to the downbeat of genesis were so appalling. As appalling as the pre-creation conditions were, in truth, the Chief Actor's production was destined to fail because of the freedom given to his co-actors. Up to this point everything had been scripted. However, from the moment the Chief Actor invited his co-actors to join him on the stage, life in the theater became risky.

Did the Chief Actor not know that the co-actors would attempt to rewrite the script, to recast their roles, and write "UNDER NEW MANAGEMENT" in bold block black letters across the doors of the theater? Of course he knew. Did the Chief Actor deterministically write the script that way? Of course not.

As the production opened all creation gathered to marvel, but more than that, to praise the Chief Actor. Everything was indeed awe-inspiring. Often in the cool of the evening the Chief Actor and his co-actors walked together. There was no agenda, no script, no rehearsals. The walks were for fellowship. The Chief Actor and his co-actors looked forward to these delightfully refreshing times of both conversation and silence. Early on, the co-actors felt that they needed to carry on a constant stream of conversation, like the life-giving river that traced through the garden before thundering over the cliff on the way to the sea. But in time the co-actors learned that just being with the Chief Actor was enough. They gained wisdom from their conversations and that was important. Such wisdom helped them fulfill their mandate. Ah, but it was in the silence, walking arm-in-arm with the Chief Actor that they gained their strength and their sense of identity. A deep bond of love formed between the Chief Actor and his co-actors.

Is it any wonder that arriving at the designated rendezvous point, a stunning, ever-in-bloom Rose of Sharon tree, that the Chief Actor was at first disappointed, then disturbed, and then terribly worried? Something awful must have befallen his co-actors. Standing alone by the Rose of Sharon, the Chief Actor shivered. Although coolness was settling in on the garden and a light breeze was beginning to pick up, this shiver came from within. It was a shiver of foreboding, a shiver of dread.

The Chief Actor called out despairingly thinking the worst, knowing the worst, yet divinely hoping for the best, "Where are you?" The pain in the voice of the Chief Actor was so poignant, so piercing, that all the created order stopped in their tracks. Deer paused with ears and tails pointing skyward. Katydids and crickets stopped their scratching. The big cats stopped their padding in midstride. Hummingbirds found a place to light.

All creation stopped and held its collective breath, for in the voice of the Chief Actor they heard the dread and pain as his question echoed through the theater of his creation, "Where are you? Where are you …? Where are …? Where …?" It was as if the Chief Actor had activated by voice the pause button on some sort of heavenly remote control. Of course no such remote was available. With formation of the co-actors, the Chief Actor gave them a free hand to create their own episodes and endings. The Chief Actor abandoned forever the possibility of remote control. He surely might have been tempted to use it if he had left himself that option.

Everything in all creation heard, including the co-actors. Taken in by the desire to receive equal, if not superior, billing with the Chief Actor, the woman and the man chose to disobey the explicit directions of the Chief Actor. Actually they thumbed their noses at the Chief Actor's blessings and prohibitions. Regarding the blessings, they didn't feel that the Chief Actor had given them everything they wished. Regarding the prohibitions, they felt that the rules and regulations, albeit very small indeed, were a burden that was chaffing their necks and strangling their freedom.

Believe it or not, it had to do with some fruit, whether to eat or not. Earlier the Chief Actor had turned over everything into their care, everything into their hands, everything, that is, except the fruit of a particular tree in the midst of the garden. "That one is not good for you. The fruit of that tree will bring about your death. Avoid it and you shall surely live."

But one of the co-actors, enticed by a talking snake, ate the forbidden fruit and convinced the other to eat as well. As soon as they had crunched into the Red Delicious apple an amazing thing occurred. The co-actors gazed upon each other, and, realizing that they were naked, rushed off to try to find something with which to cover. Fig leaves. That is all that they could find on short notice in the robing room of the garden … eating one fruit and covering with the leaves of another.

And that is where the Chief Actor found them. Huddled and hunkered down beside a fig tree trying to act cool and all together, like nothing had happened. However, the Chief Actor knew. After all, it was as plain as the looks on their faces and the fig leaves on their bodies.

"Where were you?" the Chief Actor asked again in a softer volume but no less pain ridden.

"I was naked," the male co-actor blurted out, not knowing what else to say. "I was naked," he repeated, "and when I heard you walking through the garden, I was frightened and hid!"

"How did you know that you were naked?" the Chief Actor queried. "Did you eat the fruit from the tree in the middle of the garden?"

Caught in a trap of his own making, the male co-actor knew he could not deny the obvious. And so, taking the creativity that had been given by the Chief Actor and warping it for his own advantage, he pointed to his female counterpart and said, "She gave it to me and I ate it."

Realizing she had just been fingered for the crime, the female co-actor with dramatic flare, mock sincerity, and a latent, just-under-the-surface-defiance declared, "The snake tricked me." With words she admitted her failing; after all she did eat the apple and she did convince her partner to do the same. But, in truth, her admission sounded more like an accusation. "It was the snake!" Or worse still, "You caught me red-handed and leaf-covered, but if you would have exhibited a bit more control over the details of this garden theater, none of this would have happened!" It would almost have been comical, like some Vaudevillian dialogue written to capture the delight of an audience, but it was not comical and the audience was only one, the Chief Actor himself.

When the co-actors spoke their self-scripted lines, the Chief Actor bowed his head and wept. There was a long, uncomfortable pause as if the Chief Actor had forgotten his lines. But he had not forgotten for his response had been written for this very moment. Long before the creation of the garden theater, long before his co-actors revealed their choice to disregard his love, fellowship, and wisdom, the Chief Actor had memorized his line. "The cross of Jesus," he whispered hoarsely. "This is the only way."

"We're Victims!"

Genesis 2:1-3:24

*I*t would have almost been laughable had it not been so serious, Eve and then Adam choosing to rebel, to do wrong, to sin and then trying to talk their way out of the consequences. It was while they were hiding that they began to concoct a story of deceit. They wanted to cover their tracks. No, in truth, they desired to cover their newly discovered naked backsides.

The evening breeze began to pick up. It was nearing their time of regular fellowship with God. It was a time they always treasured, but not today. As they heard God's deep voice calling out to them from the middle of the garden, Adam leaned over to Eve and said, "Remember, we're the victims here. We've got to make him believe it. All we've got to do is to both finger the serpent and we'll get off scott free. After all, are there any other witnesses?"

As God came near, he called out, "Where are you?" They knew the moment of reckoning had arrived. "Why in the world were you hiding?" God asked. The question kind of threw Adam a curve.

"We knew we were naked and so we hid ourselves," Adam said. Funny thing but that would be the last honest words that either would speak throughout the remainder of the encounter. Adam attempted to paste confidence on his face but it was not at all convincing. Eve stood just to Adam's right, a step behind, willing her knees to stop trembling.

"Who told you that you were naked?" God asked, seeing through the ruse from the very first instant. With that question Adam and Eve began to pass the buck, to evade the truth and avoid the consequences of their disastrous choices but, no matter how hard they tried, no matter what kind of garment of lies they wove together, they could not hide their guilt and shame.

An awkward silence passed. Adam was sure that God could hear the pounding of his heart and he was right. God could. Neither Adam nor Eve could look God straight in the eye. Eve mostly looked down at the ground and Adam chose to focus just off to the right of God's shoulder.

Adam spoke first. "It all began with that crafty serpent that You made," Adam said, intentionally stressing the "You" and thereby implying that God was as much to blame as the serpent was. Clearly Adam was pointing an accusing finger at God. It was not a promising beginning.

"Is that so? And just how might that be?" God queried, his questions tinged with pain, not defensiveness. But in either case the first pair was not able to pick up on God's feelings in the slightest.

Giving an amateur psychological evaluation of the serpent, Adam continued. "Apparently in the early morning light of creation that serpent of Yours was not treated as kindly or as gently by You as the other animals in the garden." Adam knew he was floundering and paused to collect his thoughts.

"Maybe the serpent was abused when he was younger," Eve inserted, trying to be helpful.

Adam gave Eve a look that let her know that she had just made a dumb comment and if he needed her help he would ask for it, thank you very much. He continued. "The serpent was neither beautiful nor useful within the animal community. He must have been made to feel worthless by the other animals. Yes, that's it: the serpent was an outcast." Adam liked where this was going. A smile. A pause. "Therefore," Adam went on, his confidence beginning to build for the first time, "the serpent was angry with You, God. He decided to make You pay a heavy price."

God listened closely. He already saw the sin, the rebellion. Adam and Eve's body language was a dead give away. God nodded his head giving the pair the freedom to continue. God was giving his highest creation the license to create. They chose to craft a lie, and it was a real whopper.

Adam needed a break. The stress of lying to the Lord of all creation was taking its toll. Eve picked up the story. "Yes, you are certainly right, my husband," nodding in his direction. "The last straw for the serpent must have been when he felt that You were playing favorites with your creation. The serpent must have been envious of Your special care and concern for us, the brightest and best of all that you made."

God wanted to be sick. Nausea rolled over him like a dark

thundercloud. He regretted the moment He had created this pair. Nevertheless He waved his hand indicating that Adam and Eve could continue.

Adam wanted to slow Eve down a bit, but she began to roll with the story. The story was taking on a life of its own. What started out as a simple double-witness accusation of the serpent blossomed into an unbelievable account that even a child could tell was far from the truth. Eve stepped out from behind the shadow of her husband and became increasingly animated. Her nervousness left her. She was center stage. The eyes of God and her husband were fastened on her. The story that poured forth was like a runaway semi careening down a steep hillside. The only place this truckload of lies was headed was for the deep ravine of judgment but Eve, and then Adam too, became caught up in the tale she was weaving. Neither saw the road ahead, so captivated were they with retelling their story.

"Resentment built up quickly in the heart and mind of the serpent. In the cool of the evening, when You were off resting ... (Not bad, Adam thought. Why not put a little more blame on God? After all, if God would have been here none of this would have happened.) an idea grew from the seed of resentment. It was a horrible idea. It was the perfect way to strike back at You and us. All night long on the seventh day the serpent pondered and strategized. By first light on the eighth day, much like the Jacaranda tree down by the spring that flowed through the garden, his plan was in full bloom."

"The Jacaranda tree is not the only thing around here that is blooming," God thought to himself, as the story of lies continued to tumble out. Yet on the face of God not the slightest indication of his anguish could be detected. A tear was forming in his eye but he brushed it away with his sleeve before either of the storytellers could notice, if they even could have noticed.

The tandem were becoming more at home in their castle of cards, their house of lies. Adam continued. "All during the morning hours the serpent methodically set in motion a plan to bring about our downfall. He hated the fact that You had said that we had been created in Your image.'"

With a strange and devilish boldness Eve ventured on, "As the serpent positioned himself this morning he couldn't help laughing to himself how You, God, overestimated your creation. 'When this day is done,' he chortled to himself, 'the Upright Ones will be down and out.'"

"Yes, 'Upright Ones', that's us, You know?" Adam interjected with a false sense of pride.

"The serpent settled into a thicket and waited," Eve went on, not really noticing Adam's interruption. She was now totally lost in her story. "I was just paying attention to the beauty of Your world, God. I was not aware that there was any danger ahead. Why should I have been? In this good world of Yours I had never felt any danger or threat."

The expression on God's face was becoming tortured but neither Adam nor Eve noticed. They were now telling their story to one another. They had become their own audience. God said nothing.

"Eve was all alone," Adam explained. "I was tilling the soil nearby, but not near enough, I guess. Apparently the serpent was counting on Eve's lack of attention and my absence. Eve was the perfect victim. As my dear wife picked flowers near the thicket, the serpent silently and slowly approached her. The serpent's slow approach was in great contrast with the blinding speed of the strike. In a flash of an eye he buried his fangs into her heel." This explanation was made using his arm as a snake and his fingers as the fangs. He flashed his fingers up toward the face of God to imitate the rapidity and ferocity of the strike.

"At first I experienced little pain," Eve said as she picked up the story. "The evil poison quickly spread through my system. As the seconds ticked by and the pain intensified, I knew that I had been victimized. The pain of this realization was almost greater than the throbbing pain of the spreading poison." These words were said in an overly dramatic fashion that would have convinced no one, especially God. Amazingly, God remained silent.

Eve rambled on. "As strange as this sounds, the poison seemed to place me under the control of the serpent. He offered me power and authority if I would entice my husband to come near the thicket and within his range. The serpent said that I would experience a kind of freedom that I had never even dreamed about. Of course without the poison I would have known that it was all a big lie, but the poison was clouding all my best thinking and righteous intent.

"I heard my wife call out, 'My love, where are you? Come and see some of God's fantastic wonders. Come here, my darling.' And so I went to where Eve was. Eve really does have a keen sense of observation, You know," Adam said as a matter of pride. "And so I went to see what Eve had discovered. She was bent over by some dainty flowers that were growing near a thicket. As Eve was chattering on about wildflowers, the serpent struck my heel. And it was just like Eve described. At first little pain but as the poison spread the pain increased. I realized I had been set up. I was a victim, too. And at that moment I fell under the spell of the vile serpent. At first I was angry. I felt betrayed," Adam said.

"Yes, and you know, I felt guilty when I saw the anger and betrayal in Adam's eyes. But that ol' serpent knew just what to do. He played on that guilty feeling over and over. He bound me up tight with guilt. He had promised freedom but we received bondage instead."

Closing with a collective sigh, Adam and Eve began to try to wheedle some sympathy out of their creator. It was to no avail. God did not buy their story. He was angered by their rebellion and hurt by their childish attempts to cover their sinfulness. God's holiness demanded that justice be done and it was swift and sure.

The serpent was punished first. God handled it quickly and directly. Then the punishment of Adam and Eve followed in short order. Before sentencing, God spoke words that were straight and true. Adam and Eve, inventors of everything that was bent and false, were forced to listen as God told them what actually happened.

"You chose to disregard my commands. You chose to go your own way. You chose to eat from the fruit of the tree that I warned you about. Although you tried to convince me that you were victims, the only ones you partially convinced were yourselves, and you didn't even do a good job at that. Deep down you know that you are not really victims of some snake-in-the-grass conspiracy." God paused to let the full weight of his words sink in. "You aren't victims at all!" God boomed.

"Sin has consequences for you and for your family. Your bold-faced lying ways will become the norm for all your children and their children's children. You have created a vast gulf between you and me. Our relationship has been broken but not because you were victims; because you willfully chose the wrong."

Pain etched the face of God. "I love you but you cannot live here any longer. I am holy and you are not. When you chose evil you chose to live outside of my presence."

As Adam and Eve trudged slowly to the edge of the garden, away from God's presence, they heard God weeping for his children, and it dawned upon them with crushing certainty that God himself was the victim, the victim of their sinfulness.

"You Mean It's Poisonous?"

Genesis 2:15-17; 3:1-24

After Adam and Eve's lungs had been filled with life, God placed them in his garden. And what a place to live! God had created this garden so that something would always be in season; cucumbers, kumquats, corn, cantaloupe – the variety was endless. Everything ripening according to God's timetable and for mankind's table. The garden was a flowering, fruit-filled paradise.

"I have given you all that you need and more," God said, his words overflowing with blessing, hope and promise.

Adam saw the distinctive tree first but it was Eve who spoke. "What about that tree over there? It is, I don't know... (she paused, almost forming the words in her mind before she spoke) tempting. Yes, tempting," she continued with a girlish laugh.

For a moment a shadow passed over the face of the Creator. Pain filled his eyes for he knew that Eve's choice of words was indeed prophetic. The smile of the father returned so quickly, in fact, that Adam and Eve never noticed. "That tree is off limits. It belongs to me."

"O.K., O.K.," Adam and Eve said in unison, sensing the command in God's voice. Adam continued, "But why? Why is that tree off limits and all the others O.K.?" It was a man-made quality that God didn't like. Instead of looking at the many that God had provided as gracious gifts and saying "Thank you," they looked at the one that God had installed as a gracious boundary and asked, "Why?"

"The why is because I love you. If you take and eat of the fruit of the tree you shall die," God answered.

"You mean it's poisonous?" Adam asked incredulously. "Why would a good God like you, the perfect Creator, plant something in your garden that is poisonous? Let's cut the sucker down and then dig out the roots!" Adam concluded expansively.

"No," God boomed. "It belongs to me and it will hurt you if you mess with it. That tree is not for your good. Trust me!"

The look in Adam and Eve's eyes sent a chill down the spine of God. It was obvious to God that simple trust had been replaced with doubt. A question had been raised in the minds of his children about his goodness, about his care. This doubt in God's goodness and care was like a welcome mat upon which the evil one would soon wipe his feet.

Adam and Eve, seeking satisfaction, pleasure and wisdom, ate of the fruit in spite of God's parental instructions. They disobeyed and were therefore banished from the garden. God now sat alone in the garden, head in his hands, and wept. Adam's question rang in his ears. "Why would a good God, a perfect Creator like you, plant something that was poisonous in the garden?"

"Because I love you and I want you to love me in return," was all that God could say.

41

God in Green Scrubs

Genesis 2:19-23

od finished up his creation. A place for everything and everything in its place. Not only did God create everything that exists, he called man and woman into existence, not as an afterthought, but as the bright and shining stars of his creation. And God did it all in almost blinding speed. He was like many parents on Christmas Eve after their children have finally been put to bed. Mom and Dad rushing around assembling bikes, placing energy cells in those toys that are clearly marked "Batteries not included," wrapping last-minute gifts in shining paper, and stuffing stockings until they are lumpy with surprises. That was the kind of feverish pace God kept up for a week. This is the fast-paced description of creation in Genesis chapter one.

The creation of man and woman as relayed in Genesis chapter two is totally different than in chapter one. Here we see the creation of humanity as if punched out, frame by frame, on God's remote control. The video player responds instantaneously. Man and woman who were called forth in his image in chapter one are now molded and formed in an amazing surgical procedure that, if repeated today, would be a shoe-in for the Nobel prize in medicine.

Of his image-bearing creation in chapter one God announces with no little pride, "This is very good!" In chapter two God is heard uttering words of frustration, "It is not good." What is it that God proclaims not good in chapter two? At this slower speed, the video clearly shows man being created before woman. God recognized that loneliness was the natural consequence of man without a suitable helper. God moves to head off the problem. God creates all kinds of spectacular, faithful and wondrous creatures. But almost the second they are created God realizes that these glorious animals will not solve man's problem of loneliness. And so, God dons his crisp green scrubs and heads for surgery. Man is anesthetized. A rib is removed and Adam's side is sutured. From this rib God miraculously fashions woman.

Man and woman are now in post-op recovering from surgery. Man comes to first and it is he, not God, who proclaims the words of blessing and appreciation over God's most recent creation. Man's words can be heard ringing down the sterile halls of Eden Surgical Hospital: "At last! Bone of my bone and flesh of my flesh. Oh thank you, God, my Creator and my Father!"

NAKED AND NOT ASHAMED

Naked and Not Ashamed

Genesis 2:25

Adam and Eve, their eldest boy, Cain, and the residents on the plain of Shinar were all visited by God. These were not joyous meetings of the fatherly Creator and his obedient children, but rather fright-filled meetings between the righteous Creator and his hand-caught-in-the-cookie jar creations.

When God went away from Adam and Eve they were naked and not ashamed. Simply put, they were innocent. They could look God in the eye. They spoke with voices of love, confidence and assurance. They belonged to God. They were loved by him. They knew they were acceptable to him. As a result they possessed great joy. Being in God's presence was the highlight of their day. When God returned, my how things had changed. God didn't need to be a genius to figure out what had happened. Adam and Eve were dressed in leaf aprons. They hid in the undergrowth at God's approach. They tended to look away when they spoke with God. Their simple love for God had been replaced with the complicated knowledge of good and evil. The confidence and assurance that once seemed bedrock to their relationship with God had vanished like the fog in the presence of the noonday sun. Their actions had made them unacceptable to God and they knew it. Hence the need for excuses. Fear had been substituted for joy. The day of God's returning created a sinking feeling in the pit of their stomachs. All they could think about was being marched off to the gallows.

And Cain, what about Cain? God had just that morning spoken with fatherly affection to his downcast Cain. In simple heavenly logic God asked, "If you do well, will you not be accepted?" Cain was in no mood to listen. Between Cain's first meeting with God and the

45

next time God approached, Cain tricked his brother into going out to an outlying field. There he killed him and buried him. Then he worked diligently to get rid of the evidence. God found Cain down by the stream trying desperately to wash the blood off his hands. But God didn't need to see the bloodstains to know what had happened. The crime was indelibly etched on the countenance of Cain. Like Adam and Eve, Cain had made a choice, a shameful choice. God knew what Cain had done and Cain knew that God knew. "Am I my brother's keeper?" was just a smokescreen, a stalling tactic until Cain could think of something better to say. He was looking for an alibi, an excuse, but he would find none. When God returned to Cain it was to pass sentence. Is that what God intended? No, indeed.

And the Shinars? These were not members of some secret society with oaths and curses. No, these people lived out on the plain. They set it in their hearts to build a tower up to the heavens, a massive structure that would be the glue to hold them together, a place of worship that would form the center of life. Deep within they knew that only God could be the true center of their lives, but they did not listen. They set out to make a name for themselves. With great industry they engineered not only a tower but also a city. But God was not impressed with their efforts. When he returned, the inhabitants were forced to flee. They became scattered over the face of the earth. The unifying

symbol of burned brick and mortar became a symbol of shame and reproach. When God came these plain dwellers could not stand in his presence.

Hearts are hungry for confidence in God's presence, for assurance of acceptability. "Do we have to live in fear of your returning, God?" people ask. We are as guilty as Adam and Eve, Cain and the Shinar Plain's people. How can we return to innocence after we have tasted the forbidden, brutalized a brother, or assigned divine status to bricks and mortar of our own making?

The good news, the response to these questions comes to us in Jesus. He is the one who allows us to stand before God with assurance that we are accepted. In a sense it is only in Jesus Christ that we can stand naked and unashamed.

"And now like little children, abide in him, so that when he is revealed we may have confidence and not be put to shame before him at his coming" (I John 2:28).

Farid Fadel

When the Hoe Handle Met the Dirt Clod

Genesis 2:8-15; 3:17-19

The wise old dirt farmer and his twelve-year-old son had worked all morning in a large parcel of cotton. Near a canal they paused for some refreshment. The father always enjoyed these times for they afforded an opportunity to hear from his son, to catch a glimpse of his soul.

On this summer morning the youngster had been particularly quiet. There had been no joy in his work. The father noticed but said nothing for he knew his son well. When the boy had pondered long enough he would speak. Not before. Still the father was puzzled. The boy was not himself. He sang none of his favorite country tunes. He hadn't stopped to examine a large colony of ants as they marched by. Nor had he tossed dirt clods into the air and hammered them for homeruns with his hoe handle.

It didn't take long for the boy to reveal his heart. "Why has God cursed us by making us work in the hot sun all day long? If it's not hoeing around cotton, it's picking it. And if not that, it's picking tomatoes or digging potatoes. Why is he cursing us?" the boy concluded with a shrug.

"Where did you get the idea that work was a curse?" the father asked with customary patience.

"Last night mama was reading from the Bible. She read about God cursing Adam with this kind of back-breaking work." He ventured ahead with his thought. "I guess God had the right to curse Adam but why did he have to curse us, too?"

"Oh, my son," the father said, "I don't think you heard all of what mama read last night. Before the curse part God gave Adam words of purpose and blessing." The father recited the passage from Genesis from memory as if he had this conversation with himself and studied

49

the matter closely. "Now the Lord God had planted a garden in the east, in Eden; and there he put the man he had formed…The Lord took the man and put him in the Garden of Eden to work it and take care of it."

"Work is not a curse, my boy. Work came before the curse." As the father spoke he gently fingered some of the soil in his hand. "We have the opportunity," the father continued slowly, "to plant the seed and see those seeds peek their heads up through the soil. We help God water them and later we harvest them." His voice was filled with such love. . . awe, really.

The boy sat amazed. His burden had been strangely lifted. God was not cursing him. That was enough for him to know. He honestly didn't understand it. Work was still work, and to him, sometimes, it still felt like a curse. But his father spoke with such love and faith he couldn't help being convinced. He hugged his father tightly.

As if energized by love the youngster picked up his hoe and began to be radio announcer, manager, fan, and hero at the plate — all rolled into the mind, body and soul of a twelve-year-old boy. He tossed the dirt clod high into the air with a swing that Barry Bonds would have been proud of. His skinny-handled hoe connected with the clod. The radio announcer told the world of the massive shot. The hero stood at the plate and marveled at the blast. And the father smiled.

Fall in the Meadow

Genesis 3:14-19

t was a lovely green meadow just beyond the borders of an amazingly lush garden. All the trees and flowers that circled the meadow were in full bloom, or at least had recently been in full bloom. Really they were a day or two past full bloom. The meadow and its surroundings looked like a gorgeous carnation boutonnière after a summer's wedding. This carnation had been out of the florist's cooler for quite some time now. It was a very thirsty-looking flower, a bit rumpled from all the banging it had received as person after person in the receiving line had hugged the groom. The meadow had that certain used look. From a distance everything was perfect. Yet, on closer inspection, the greenery in this meadow was beginning to wrinkle and shrivel at a frightening rate. Colors were changing. Brown was becoming more prominent. The courtroom was located in this meadow just to the east of the fertile garden.

Yesterday the crime had been committed. This morning at the trial the verdict had been announced. "Guilty as charged" rang through the meadow. The sentencing was scheduled for mid-afternoon.

The case against the man and the woman was the first judicial case in history. The courts were not overcrowded, as yet. And jails were non-existent. To be sure, the days of jammed court dockets and jails bursting at the seams with prisoners were just around the corner.

The man and the woman had been accused and found guilty of grand theft, falsification of records, and attempting to impersonate God.

The sun had passed its zenith and was beginning its gradual decline toward the west. The time for sentencing was just moments away. The courtroom was packed with observers. There was a deadly hush as if the sentence passed on this young couple would have a spillover effect on the rest of creation.

51

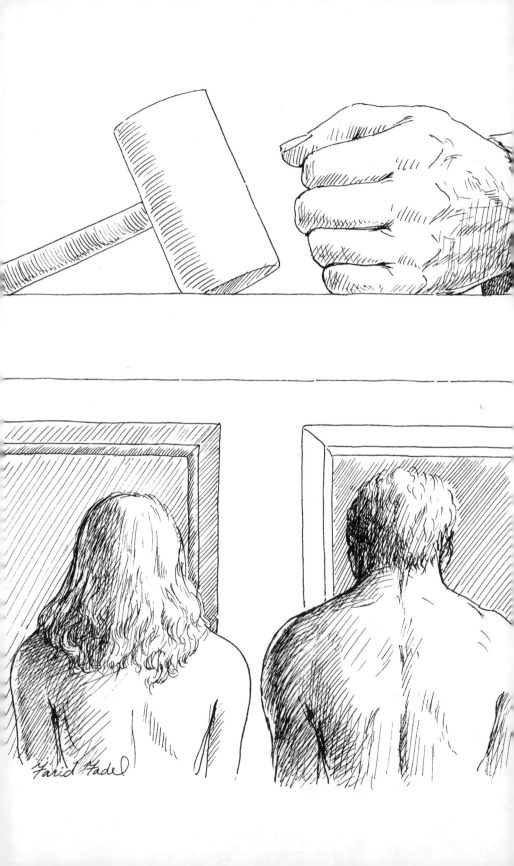

The serpent had been sentenced at high noon. The judge had been particularly harsh. The serpent had been cast out of the garden. As surely as he now stood in the meadow it was clear to all that he would never reenter the garden of paradise. The world outside the garden would be a place where he would be eternally hunted. The serpent would strike back often with deadly accuracy. Yet in the end he was destined to be stomped to death.

The serpent didn't have a leg to stand on; his defense had been so weak at his trial. As if to make that abundantly clear to all creation, the serpent's limbs were amputated. Never again would he run. He was forced to slither through life licking up the dust.

What would the sentence be on this young couple? Some believed that they had been duped by the serpent, like they were pawns in some universal power struggle between good and evil. But the evidence that had been presented in the meadow court that morning proved beyond the shadow of a doubt that both the man and the woman had intentionally chosen to break the law, to spit in the face of the creator.

The judge entered the meadow. As he did, a chilling wind began to blow. Nothing like that had ever happened in or near the garden. The man and the woman shivered, an involuntary reaction to the wind and the stern expression on the face of the judge. The judge stood in the center of the meadow and the couple folded before him.

With little introduction the judge began the proceedings. The time for sentencing had come. Off in the distance a woodpecker hammered out a steady beat, a drum roll.

To the woman first: "This court has found you guilty of all three charges against you. Therefore, after consulting in triune holiness, this court issues the following sentence:

> In pain you shall bring forth children and
> in greater agony you shall be forced to
> raise them in the fallen world that you
> have so intentionally created. Also, since
> you have turned away from God to your husband
> the result shall be that he will often take
> great advantage of you. You are hereby
> expelled from the garden. Ultimately you
> will die as a direct result of your crime."

To the man: "This court has found you guilty of all three charges against you. Therefore, after consulting in triune holiness, this court issues the following sentence:

> In great frustration you shall work. Your
> greatest aspirations for success and
> satisfaction will be thwarted. Hope will
> never leave you that this year's crop
> will be better than the last. But
> harvest after harvest you will be sorely
> disappointed. Thorns and thistles will
> grow wild as you attempt to scratch out a
> meager existence for you and your family.
> You are hereby expelled from the garden.
> Ultimately you will die as a direct result
> of your crime."

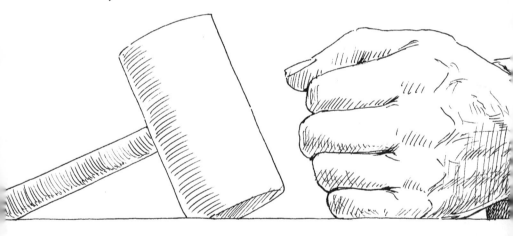

The sentence was passed. In stunned silence the young couple left the meadow courtroom. As they walked away the wind picked up again. A frost could be seen forming on the meadow's grasses. The pungent smell of decaying leaves was in the air. Eve shivered again as Adam tried unsuccessfully to warm her under his arm.

The judge called for the couple to stop and in mercy issued them clothing of animal skins. They would need some protection against the weather. Fall had come to the meadow and beyond and winter was not far away.

Angel at the Gate

Genesis 3:24

The siren screamed through heaven. It was a call to arms. Angels raced to and fro, although in a highly organized manner. They had been in a heightened state of readiness since Satan had deceived "The Couple," as the heavenly hosts called them.

The angel cohorts assembled in God's judgment hall. They were an impressive corps. All were dressed in uniform fashion: long dazzling white robes with golden sashes across their chests. Strapped to their waists were gleaming swords which when unsheathed flamed to life. In their left hands were shields of burnished bronze and their feet were shod with golden sandals, stronger than tank treads, swifter than Reeboks. The uniform was completed with shining headgear. Their appearance bespoke power, authority, invincibility and holiness.

As God entered the judgment hall this vast army snapped to attention, as if one.

The question on everyone's mind was this: "Is now the time we are going to defeat Satan?" Surely God intended on rooting out this cancerous enemy before he polluted the entirety of God's marvelous creation.

The room was tense with emotion. The angels were straining with desire, the desire for battle. Although at attention, one could see the bands of muscles in their necks and arms were taut, steel-like. Their eyes blazed with holy fury. Their expressions were fixed. They were at the extreme edge of readiness. All attention was focused on the holy Creator, the righteous judge.

As God stood before his crack troops, he was silent. He visibly reviewed his troops as surely as if he passed before them one-by-one, staring into their souls. No one squirmed. They were wholly and holy

ready for his penetrating gaze. He studied those assembled with minute care, as if he were determining the one he would dispatch on a mission of extreme urgency. And indeed he was. God was not rushed nor did he appear anxious. Just the opposite. He was deliberate and confident.

Then God spoke. It was the same voice that called forth the world from a blackened tangle of chaos. It was a majestic voice. It was the unimagined power dressed in words. The omnipotent God answered the question on everyone's mind. "I do not authorize you to destroy Satan at this time!" A collective gasp escaped from the assembled angelic army. The gasp almost thundered. God was not in the habit of explaining his battle plans to his troops and he didn't start now. "Today," God continued, "I have expelled man and woman from my garden." Another gasp. All of heaven knew that God had created humankind a little lower than they themselves. He had crowned them with glory and honor. He had subjected everything under their feet. Not only that, but each and every angel knew of God's intense love for man and woman.

God's white-hot gaze scanned the ranks before him. Without delay God called the name Flavious, an angel who stood smartly at his right hand. "Your assignment is to block the gate, the gate of return into the garden. Your assignment is exceedingly important. If man and woman are allowed to reenter the garden and eat from the Tree of Life they will be forced to live forever in their sin." The significance of the task crashed upon Flavious and on all the other angels, as well.

God spoke again, this time more to his son than to the angels. "No, we shall not destroy Satan at this time. I have an eternally victorious plan, but this is not the moment to put it into effect." The angels did not understand God's words. But father and son understood. Yes, the son understood the painful and yet triumphant implications of God's words completely.

Thus the angel Flavious, flaming sword in hand, was dispatched to stand at the gate.

The Gargoyles Laughed

Genesis 4:1-16

*F*orced to leave the job he knew best, forced to leave the parents that reared him, forced to leave the protection of the familiar, Cain plodded out into the dusty, uncharted and barren wasteland of his own making. Cain stumbled through the gate into Nod.

What frightened Cain most about this far-from-a-fairyland place? Leaving family didn't bear mentioning. Being expelled from his source of livelihood made his heart skip a beat. But it was the two gargoyles perched on the medieval-looking tower that marked the entrance to Nod that unnerved him.

The ghoulish glance of the first gargoyle set utter terror loose in Cain's soul. Cain was being forced to leave the presence of God. Cain knew in the bottom of his wildly-beating heart that God wanted what was best for him. After all, why had God come to speak with him so frankly before he committed the well-planned murder of his younger, well-respected brother? Cain had thought out everything – everything, that is, except the consequences of his actions. Or perhaps Cain had thought them out, too, and believed he could live with them. The fact was, now that he had bludgeoned his brother to death, the verdict "Guilty as charged" and the sentence "Banishment from the presence of God" were too much for him to bear.

The gargoyle on the right seemed to smirk with evil delight as he spoke. "God never wants to see your ugly, sinful face again. You belong in Nod. You have always been destined for Nod." A shrill laugh escaped the gargoyle's thin stone lips.

Cain's mouth dropped and his shoulders sagged noticeably. "Banishment. Have I really been on the road to Nod all my life? Was I created for this hell?"

Before he could answer his own question, Cain spied the second gargoyle, the one with a twisted, gruesome expression. A spasm of horror swept through him. The question of the gargoyle on the left was issued in hissing tones. "What if some of Abel's children seek revenge?" Clawing at his own eyes with needle-pointed fingers the gargoyle shrieked, "An eye for an eye and a tooth for a tooth!"

Cain passed under the gargoyle as he entered the land of Nod. He instinctively looked over his shoulder to see if someone was lurking in the shadows. A cold damp mist seemed to box him in.

Nod was a dark dreary place where people continually stumbled over the consequences of their own sins. It was a most frightening place because it was here that people like Cain got the self-inflicted punishment they so richly deserved. Nod was like an island of desolation where regret and the fear of retribution were the twin fires that lick at the garbage men and women have made of their lives.

The fear, regret, and isolation, combined with the demonic atmosphere of Nod, were more than Cain could bear. "My punishment is greater than I can stand!" As a result, God placed on Cain his mark, a coat-of-arms, so to speak, of the family of God. The mark was highly visible yet it did not disfigure. The message was clear. "If you touch Cain, you will have to deal with God."

God spoke to Cain. "I never said you were forced from my presence. You said it. I didn't." God reached out his nail-scarred hands in forgiveness. Cain couldn't hear. The wind off the plain of Nod whistled in Cain's ears. Cain trudged into the land of wandering, the evil land of his own making. And the gargoyles laughed.

Retaliation or Forgiveness

Genesis 4:17-24

amech must have been a good father. When his first son, Jabal, grew interested in animals, Lamech encouraged him to join the local 4-H club. Lamech was there when Jabal won first prize at the county fair. He stood by Jabal's side through the black of the night when Jabal nursed his prize-winning calf back to health. When Jabal exceeded his father's level of expertise with animals, Lamech was not threatened in the least. In fact, it was Lamech who encouraged his son to get a degree in Animal Husbandry from Eastern Eden University. At Jabal's graduation Lamech was first in line to congratulate his son.

Jubal, Lamech's second son, was always interested in music. As a boy Jubal was always banging on some pot or pan, blowing on a homemade reed flute, or organizing the neighbor kids into some kind of orchestra. Later when Jubal joined the Marching Eagle band of Enoch High, Lamech was at every marching contest and half-time show. Lamech was in the audience for the initial performance of the "Jubalaires," a panpipe and lyre quintet that Jubal had formed. No father could have been prouder and no one in the audience applauded longer. It was a stunning arrangement of "All Things Bright and Beautiful," arranged, of course, by Jubal.

Tubal-cain, the third son, also received his father's encouragement. He attended the area-wide Vocational Technical High School. Almost all of Tubal-cain's ("TC" to his friends) courses were in pre-engineering. At graduation a local construction firm offered the boy a job as a civil engineer, but he turned the job offer down. Instead, TC opened a blacksmithing establishment next to the livery at the edge of Enoch. Lamech, although disappointed, never let his son know. In fact, Lamech was one of the key backers and shareholders in the blacksmith shop.

The boy had been teased that TC stood for "Too Chubby" when he was younger. TC had always been a bit on the husky side. By high school there was little that could be called chubby about the boy. He had become a small mountain. He was big and he was strong. He became a wrestler, a state champion on a championship team. At those state championships an incident happened that would affect Lamech and his family immensely; like pouring vinegar in sweet milk, the incident had a curdling effect.

In the parking lot after the finals, Lamech was out celebrating the team's victory with some of the other men from around Enoch. A young man, a kid really, started taunting them, telling them that the team from the Vo-Tech would never have won had they not bought off the referee. Lamech answered back and soon a shouting match had broken out. But Lamech tired of the foolishness. After all, he knew that his team, and more importantly, his son, was state champion and nothing this kid could say or do could change that. "Why don't you go back home to your mama's teats, boy? I think I hear her squealing for her baby piglet," Lamech shouted as he turned to leave. He and the men with him howled with laughter. Something in the boy snapped. No doubt it was the reference to his mother being a sow that did it. The boy picked up a discarded beer bottle and charged Lamech. With a hammering blow the young man broke the bottle across the back of Lamech's head. Blood splattered everywhere. Lamech saw red. He went to his car and picked out one of Tubal-cain's sharpest iron tools. He hunted down the boy in the crowds and murdered him.

The people from Enoch said that Lamech was well within his rights to do such a thing. The family of the dead boy vowed revenge. "We have very long memories," they shouted with clenched fists.

When Lamech returned home he still had dried blood, both his own and the boy's, on his hands. He gathered his two wives and children around him and told them what had happened. "If anyone tries to kill me or mine, let it be known that this family will avenge it. If they kill one of ours we will kill seventy-seven of theirs!" The family knew that Lamech meant it. There was not a shred of exaggeration in his voice.

The feuding, bloodletting, and retaliation that began that day continues to this.

Some just shake their heads and say "That's life." Not Jesus. Instead of retaliation up to seventy-seven times, Jesus called for forgiveness in like proportions.

Being Born in the Likeness of Adam

Genesis 4:25-5:8

dam and Eve were devastated by the murder of Abel. Adam grieved silently. Eve entered a period of severe depression. She sat alone in her tent day after day racked with great sobs; her tears had long ago dried up. It wasn't just the death of Abel, but also God's expulsion of Cain. Over and over again Eve would moan, "On the same day I lost both of my sons. On the same day I lost both of my sons."

Two years passed before Eve would allow Adam to even touch her. With time came some small amount of healing, a tiny scab was forming over the vast open wound of her grief. Soon both Adam and Eve were convinced that the only way true healing would come to their ravaged souls was if laughter would return to their tent. "Laughter," Adam counseled, "is the by-product of children." And so, in a lusting sort of way, Adam and Eve set about to get pregnant. They were not lusting for one another as they had done long ago; now they lusted for a child, a child of healing. Within a few weeks after they began trying to conceive, Eve was certain she was pregnant. Joy began to sprout its head amidst the soil of their marriage relationship, a soil that had been fertilized by pain, tilled by disappointment and watered by tears.

Adam left the name giving to Eve. He said to himself, "Her pain has been so great. I have only experienced the ragged edges of her heart-wrenching pain." After Eve gave birth it took four days before she settled on a name. She called the baby boy Seth because "God has appointed me another child instead of Abel, because Cain killed him." She told this to Adam.

When friends and neighbors came by to see the new baby everyone remarked how much Seth took after his daddy. "You have a 'keeper'," one neighbor said pounding Adam on the back. "He looks just like you, papa!"

Adam had seen his likeness in the boy from the first — the ruddy complexion, dark eyes, the cleft chin, the stocky build. As Seth grew Adam saw more of his image than he would have liked. He saw rebellion and self-centeredness. He saw a proud, almost haughty attitude. He saw great potential enslaved in this maturing body of his third son, Seth.

Some said it was only natural that Seth would grow up this way. Eve had always protected and sheltered the boy. She would forever be afraid of suffering the loss of Seth, a loss she knew she would be unable to bear.

Adam was now older, much older. Eve had died more than twenty summers ago. She had lived to see her great-great grandchildren. Adam and Seth still looked very much alike — same walk, same manner of talking, same balding pattern. As Adam reflected on his life, a startling thought struck him. Adam had been created in the image of God, in the likeness of the Creator. Seth, as a result of Adam's sin, had been created in his image. When Adam looked at Seth, the ancient one was forced to repent because he now knew that he had replaced God's perfect image with a broken-mirrored reflection. Seth and all his children's children were forced to pay a heavy price. They would be born in the likeness of Adam, a tarnished imitation of the image God had given to him.

Relief

Genesis 5:28-29

Lamech had just left the field. The sweat rolled down the canyon in his back. His hands were calloused. His muscles ached. The dust and dirt clung to his sweaty frame.

"All this work and so little to show for it," he thought. The fig trees didn't blossom this year and there was no fruit on the vines. The olive crop was a dismal failure. "What would they do if the olive crop failed?" he wondered. It was a bleak year for just about everything, except for weeds. It was a bumper crop for thorns and thistles.

"Milk, what I wouldn't do for some cistern-cooled milk." For some reason the thought of milk made Lamech think of his wife who was heavy with child. "Heavy with child," he thought. "What a crazy way to talk about a pregnant woman. Heavy? She's not heavy. She looks like a fresh wine skin that is ready to burst." A smile creased his face.

A child. They had waited so long. In spite of being bone-weary, a little skip broke his stride. "God," he prayed, "give me a son."

Fatigue settled in on him. It seemed to descend from his head and shoulders and when it crashed upon his feet he staggered, unable to stand. He slouched down beside the road. He couldn't make it up the last hill toward his home. "What shall I name this child?" he thought. But he was too tired and hungry to concentrate.

He couldn't move a muscle, that is, until he saw the midwife flying to meet him. "Lamech, Lamech," she cried breathlessly, "you have a son!"

65

Fatigue vanished. Joy returned. Lamech was beside himself. He bounded up the hill, praises on his lips. As he pushed through the door he heard a lusty wail. Lamech rushed to his wife's side. The boy was already drinking heartily from his mother's breast. Lamech, as many a new father since that time, was overcome by the wonder of new life. He plopped down on the stool near his wife's head. He bent over and kissed her. Oh how he appreciated that woman who had put up with him and her "barren standing" in the community for so long. "I love you," he whispered taking her hand.

Later the child slept. "Do you want to hold him, papa?" Lamech's wife asked with a tender smile. Although exhausted, Lamech lifted himself from his stool and picked up the sleeping child. Gently he sat down, the child nestled in the crook of his arm. A tear rolled down his cheek and dropped on the baby's white wrappings.

"What shall I name you, little one?" Lamech asked softly. He had no answer for the moment. "Oh God," Lamech prayed, "take this child and use him. Make him a blessing."

Lamech slept with the child in his arms. How long he slept he really didn't know. Lamech was now awake. Although he was still tired he was able to focus his thoughts. Lamech reviewed his day of frustration and fatigue. He marveled at how the news of the birth of his son had given his worn-out body relief. "That's it!" he said looking down at his sleeping son. "I know your name. I'll call you Noah." It was a name, a prayer, and a prophecy.

He named him Noah saying, "Out of the ground that the Lord has cursed, this one shall bring us relief from our work and from the toil of our hands."

BILLY ANGEL

Billy Angel

Genesis 6:1-7

When Billy Angel was sixteen years of age his mother divorced his father and moved away. Billy chose to live with his father. Billy knew very little about his folks except that they had had a very unhappy marriage for as far back as he could remember. His folks came from different social and religious backgrounds. They came from different worlds, literally. Seldom did his folks have a civil word for each other. Billy's dad spoke often of his "big regret." The words were like a hammer to his mother. Eventually her shame and soul-sickness drove her away. Where she went no one knew. She just seemed to vanish.

What Billy knew was this: when Billy's dad first laid eyes on his mother he determined to marry her. He gave up everything to do so. It was the perfect love story. Growing up, Billy often wondered why this perfect love story didn't seem to be heading for a happy ending, let alone a happy middle.

Billy's dad never spoke of what he had given up in order to marry his mother. It was too painful. Billy knew that this had everything to do with his father's "big regret," but he was never quite able to pull all the pieces together.

Billy's dad used to be an angel, a personal servant of the God of the universe, the creator of everything, the Lord of all. What Billy's dad had given up to come to earth was meaning and purpose. He had given up right standing before God himself. Billy's dad tried to cover his sense of failure and loss with alcohol. He was a drunk. On rare occasions when he was sober he would tell Billy about the "good ol' days." These were the glory days. Billy loved these stories.

Billy's dad could speak for hours about the glories of heaven and the splendor of God's throne room. When his dad spoke, Billy sat enthralled, hanging on every word. Billy lived to hear stories his dad

68

would speak about God, his creative genius, his righteous judgments, and his marvelous power. What Billy's dad spoke about most, however, were his friends among the angel guard. Never had his dad had truer friends. Never had friends been more faithful. In Billy's eyes everything on earth paled by comparison.

Once when Billy was caught-away in the wonderful stories of heaven he asked his father, "Why did you do it, Dad? Why did you leave all that?"

Billy's dad tried to explain. In a moment of rare disclosure, rare honesty, he tried to answer for his son the question that had plagued him for years. "I left," Billy's dad began with great hesitation, "because I wanted your mother more than I wanted God."

"Couldn't you have both?" Billy asked.

"No, son, I couldn't." He breathed a huge sigh and continued into territory he had never intended to enter with anyone, let alone his son. "I gave up everything. I gave up my standing with God…" his voice trailed off. "You see, son, I forced your mother to sleep with me. It wasn't her idea. It was mine. You are the result of that, that (searching for the right word)… relationship." That didn't sound right so he tried again. "Son, I raped your mother and she became pregnant. You are that child," he finished bluntly.

The words stung and made sense all at the same time. All the comments at school. All the jokes. His parents' bad marriage. His father's regret. His mother's shame. How could he have been so blind? "Billy Angel, illegitimate child." The words banged in his ears with each heartbeat. He was the child of one of the sons of God and one of the daughters of Eve.

The news destroyed Billy Angel. Some say that the truth hurts but in time there is healing. The healing never came for Billy. Trying to find acceptance he followed his father's example – alcohol. Women, many women, came later. Billy also followed his mother's example. He left home. No one heard about Billy Angel in those parts for many years.

Billy Angel became a great soldier. He didn't fear death. This always amazed his companions. He seemed to live and fight as though defying death and inviting it at the same time. He became a warrior of great renown. Many legends grew up about Billy Angel. Perhaps the last one is the saddest. Legend tells us that when the rains began and the floodwaters came over the earth, Billy Angel tried to lead an armed takeover of the ark. Billy Angel died trying.

Heroes and warriors? Our children need parents whose marriages are without regret and shame. May we as parents be this kind of hero. May we be the kind of warriors who stand against evil and do battle in the power of the Name.

Billy Angel? Whether we like it or not, our children get a steady diet of such "great men of renown" outside our homes. Let us work to redefine the words *hero* and *warrior* for our children.

The Day God Stormed "Enough!"

Genesis 6:1-8

ime. God created it. He made a way to measure it. "Sun to mark the day and a moon to mark the night." He had said it and it was so. Spacious sky and spatial earth were formed not in a crucible but as the very syllables of creative thought rolled off the tongue of God. At God's call, dry land propped itself up on its elbows and made itself visible in the midst of the waters. Green patches began to burst forth, and before long glorious blossoms dangled and danced at the ends of vines and branches. And animals? Striped, spotted and solid-colored, they began darting and charging about; the turtle and the slough darted and charged but in a slower fashion than the gazelle or the leopard. Birds of all shapes and sizes filled the air and nested in the verdant foliage. All this creative energy was not done willy-nilly fashion. Certainly not! It was at the very command of God, as if God were directing and producing a vast play of universal proportions.

At some sort of divine cadence God announced the goodness of all that he had created. If there had been any observers during creation week, they would have seen and heard the divine blessing, "That's good!" Sometimes this blessing was almost shouted out in pride and at other times it was whispered in delicate pleasure.

But all that had gone before was almost nothing compared to the creative resonance that rose in God's voice as he said, "Let's make man in our own image." The gentle breeze stopped blowing and the dangling flowers, as a result, stopped dancing. Animals stood still in their tracks. The waves rolled up ready to crash upon the shore but then suspended themselves in midair. Nothing happened. No sound. No movement. Nothing but a holy hush. Creation was standing on tiptoe waiting to see God call forth his image. And he did! And God was obviously pleased. The breeze caressed the faces of man and woman. The trees and plants began to burst forth with fruits and vegetation in expectation of humankind's need for food. The animals rushed to circle the legs of man and woman like a loving house pet. And the waves? They crashed and roared to the shore in a riotous standing ovation to the Creator and the masterpiece of creation. And God, although almost speechless in wonder himself, after a brief moment proudly announced, "Now this piece of creation is VERY GOOD!" God was bursting his buttons and deservedly so.

As the time that God had created ticked on, a shadow fell over God's good globe. God, the master spokesman of creation, stuttered in disbelief as his most precious creation chose to turn away. Humankind with free choice had chosen another master. And God, the one who spoke these priceless treasures into existence, was now forced to speak words of judgment. The words were uttered under extreme duress. Enmity, pain, sweat, fruitless toil and death were almost whispered into creation. God the Creator was choked with emotion.

Things seemed to spin recklessly out of control. With each sunset and waning moon the created treasures, humankind, wandered farther and farther away. In a moment of rage one of man's children began and completed a horrible creation himself. Murder was born. God was dumbstruck. All he could manage to say was, "Where is your brother?" Pain caved in upon the Creator. Man's child created the smart-aleck response, "Am I my brother's keeper?" God was stunned. "What have you done?" The words tumbled out from the same lips that had very recently formed "Very Good!"

Now one thing that God was sure of was that humankind was living too long. He could barely stand their swaggering pride. Humility was not a word humankind had chosen to invent and they were even less intent on modeling it. God stated his verdict. "One hundred and twenty years; and that is it. If man can't find a way to me in one hundred and twenty years I simply won't wait any longer."

The word *Enough* was forming in the creative recesses of God's mind. "Perhaps I have made a mistake?" God began to regret his creative burst of energy during the week of beginnings that now seemed so long ago.

The seed of evil was now planted and humankind was intent on watering it. Wickedness flourished. Man and woman thought only about evil and how to accomplish it in every vile, immediate and pleasurable way possible. Where humankind had once sought out God's presence, they began to long for the cover of darkness to accomplish their evil desires. Soon it didn't matter. Darkness or daylight, doing evil was the solid focus of their thought and actions.

Another sunset. . . another full moon. The creator was transformed from a grieving father into a wrath-filled judge. "The time has come to blot out this mess!" he thundered. Again creation stood still. Man lifted his head from the breast of the prostitute. The thief paused in the middle of his break-in. The mother's hand stopped in mid-air, the smoldering twig poised and ready to make another burn on her child's skin. The miser stopped counting his ill-gotten gain. The child's vulgar and abusive torrent was cut in mid-stream. The one word that all feared was about to be proclaimed. God was about to wipe creation away. The word flooded through God's lip. "ENOUGH!"

As soon as God said it his eye fell on Noah. The creative mind that placed electric currents in lightning bolts and speckled trout in streams began to muse again. Redemptive creation. "What if I made a covenant? Now is the time to use one righteous man if there ever was one." The day God said "Enough" was the day he reconsidered because Noah found favor in the creative gaze of God. In fact, it was Noah that sparked the creative imagination of God. At that moment in time God saw a craft, a ship with an eight-member crew, none of whom knew the least thing about seamanship. A smile broke out on God's face. It was the first smile that God had smiled since Enoch had walked with him, and that seemed like a long time ago. The sternness was shattered. "What about the animals?" God thought. "Will I destroy them all as if I were a child throwing a tantrum? No, I will save them; I will rescue my creation. Hey, a floating zoo!" In spite of himself, God laughed. It was a good laugh, a healing laugh.

The rains came; the storm progressed from sprinkle to deluge in no time at all. But in the midst of the judgment, God's mighty rescue was in operation.

And to think it all happened, such joy-filled imaginings, on the same day when God finally lost his patience. The day God stormed 'Enough!"

The Calm, The Dream, and The Wind

Genesis 6:1-8:1

The Calm...

In forty days, by way of a storm of hurricane proportions, God totally destroyed his creation. He blotted out everything, everything except those of us on the ark.

And then it stopped. The sun came out. At first we were thrilled. Our salvation was in sight. God had fulfilled his promise. We were safe atop the waters. I found a piece of coal and began recording my praises on the walls. We were thankful. We were content for we knew that we were in God's hands as surely as we were in this floating cypress-wood craft.

Day twenty-five since the storm stopped. We are all doing our chores. No one seems to be laughing much.

Day thirty-nine. The infection in Ham's foot is sending red streaks up his leg. He is keeping his foot elevated.

Day fifty-three. Tired of the smell. It stinks so bad you can hardly sleep, let alone eat.

Day seventy-five. We are locked in a period of unending calm. Everyone is tense. No one is speaking to each other. Even the animals seem to lash out at each other.

Day ninety-two. Still in the calm. No wind. No breeze. No movement of air of any kind. Flies are multiplying.

Day one hundred and twenty-one. Will we ever see land again? What is God's plan? He saved us from the hecklers and the storm. Now he lets us languish on the water.

Day one thirty-seven. Having to ration fresh water. Does anyone know how much water a camel can drink at one setting? This isn't funny!

Day one forty-nine. Has God forgotten us?

Noah drops the piece of coal and crumples with a thud. It's day 149 since the storm. Noah and his family are very discouraged. Nothing on the horizon. The sea that once boiled with God's rage has calmed. It's a deathly calm. A boring calm. The kind of calm that drives you insane.

Noah is slouched in the corner of the cabin he calls home. His hair is matted. His spirit is as tattered as his clothes. He is a ragged, beaten man. "How," he wonders, "did I ever end up here? Would that I had died with the rest of God's creation. Is this some sort of a cruel joke?"

The Dream...

Sleep finally comes. A deep sleep. A sleep of dreams.

Zee-zaw. Zee-zaw. Zee-zaw. Twang-zaugh . . . snap! That was the eighth time since he had begun this crazy project that his saw blade had snapped. Noah lost his patience. And besides that his hands still hurt. Oh sure, the bleeding had stopped but the meaty portions of his hands still looked more like bloody sacrifices than work-toughened leather.

Noah plopped down on a cypress stump, one of the very few he had managed to create since he began this backbreaking work three weeks ago. "I'm not a lumberjack," he thought for the hundredth time that afternoon. "How did I get myself into this?" he asked. It wasn't a question that searches for an answer. It was more of a question asked out of frustration. Yes, that was it exactly. Noah was deeply frustrated and he had no one to complain to.

Was it really possible that three weeks ago and a day, near this very spot while Noah rested, that God had approached him? "What was it I was thinking about?" he wondered out loud. "I remember. I was concerned about my sons. Growing up these days. It was hard enough when I was young. But now . . . violence and perversion and unimaginable wickedness seem not only to be the talk of the town but the activity of the town, as well. I was asking God for a solution, a way out." He remembered his exact words. "God, couldn't you send some sort of revival? No one seems to remember you as the Creator of every good and perfect gift. Your name seems to be relegated to cursing and swearing only. Won't you do something?"

That was when God responded. There was such frustration in his voice. Yes, it was frustration. Noah knew frustration. He glanced over at the saw blade. But his frustration was nothing like the frustration that he heard in God's voice. And there was pain there, too. And anger. God said that he was going to destroy everything.

At this point Noah really wasn't sure he was hearing from God. He thought maybe he had swallowed some bad water. Maybe it was the onions and leeks that he had at lunch. Indigestion? Hallucinations? No, it was God. Noah was sure of it. But what God commissioned him to do – "far-fetched" was a mild way to put it. Yet there was a constant theme in what God said. "You and your family, I'm going to save."

Sometimes Noah's sons came home after working in the town and told him about the villager's comments. Noah knew they talked about him. This talk embarrassed his children. People said that Noah walked with God. Someone even told the oldest boy that when Noah went to sleep at night he better tie his father's feet to the bedpost. If he didn't do that, the man said, the boys might end up without a pa. They said it happened to ol' Enoch and it might happen to their crazy old man. Shem was really angry at the way the men in the store had howled with laughter.

"What would those townsfolk think about me right now?" Noah wondered in the midst of the dream. "Out here in the middle of a cypress swamp, miles from any kind of major waterway, building an ark. An ark? That is what God had said. I didn't even know what an ark was." As God explained, an ark was a BIG BOAT. Three decks tall. A roof on it. Hundreds of cubits long. Fifty cubits wide. Thirty tall. All Noah knew was that was a lot of cypress wood! Noah looked down again at his discarded saw and then focused on his painful hands.

And Noah was supposed to collect animals, male and female. A whole bunch of them. In fact, God said male and female of every kind that he had made. "Give me a break! Here I am still trying to saw down cypress trees — maybe I have enough wood for the gang-plank — and I'm supposed to turn from being a shipbuilder to being a zoologist? I'm going home. This kind of thinking wears me out more than the sawing."

As Noah slowly walked home he thought of telling his boys. "I've got to do it," he said. God had said his family was to join him on this boat. "Me and the Mrs. and the boys and their wives," he mumbled to himself. "Anyway, I've got to tell them. I can't build this boat by myself. And collect the animals. And get them all aboard. And gather food. And get it all aboard." He thought about how hungry he was.

"Noah, are you listening? You and your boys, their wives and yours. I'm going to save them."

That night when Noah gathered his family everyone seemed to take the news better than Noah had imagined. It was such a wild story. But they believed him. They actually believed that God had spoken to him. All but the youngest. He kind of scoffed a bit. "And just what is God gonna do while we're sawing and slaving, herding and harvesting?" The tension was broken when Noah chuckled and said, "God says he's gonna provide the water." Everyone started to laugh. The way Japheth was cutting up, Noah knew he was with them. They laughed that night until they cried.

From that point on the eight family members worked as a team. They labored and toiled in an almost endless fashion. News was soon to leak out about what was taking place down in the cypress swamp. The boat was beginning to take shape, although Noah had to admit that it looked more like a three-story barn than it did a boat. Noah and his boys would be careful to build it to the specs, God's specifications. And with every cut of the saw and every bang of the hammer Noah heard God rehearsing his promise. "You and your family, I am going to save."

People would gather from miles around to jeer at them. Some young poet in the crowd started the chant and it became kind of the crowd's theme song of mockery.

"Gonna build a boat?
    Gonna make it float?
        Gonna dig a moat?
            Where's the water?"

Noah and his family quickly grew sick of hearing those words!

At night they had to stand guard lest someone sabotage their work. In the darkness of the night the crickets and crackling fire seemed to remind Noah of God's promise. "I'm going to rescue you from among the people. I have a purpose for you."

Somehow the women were able to plant and care for a massive crop of grain. The men took off several days to help bring it in. In the odd moments everyone gathered berries, nuts, vines, and tubers.

Noah huddled into a ball. He pulled some more straw around him for warmth. The dream, although disrupted, continued.

There they were. Noah and the boys building the ark. It took a long time. Toward the end of the building process Noah mounted his donkey in search of animals to take on the voyage. He did it on a regular basis as the boat began to progress. Some people think that all those animals lived right there in the cypress swamp. Not so. And it wasn't like Noah could reason with the animals. It didn't stop him from trying however. It took a great effort to convince a couple of rhinos that it was in their best interest to come along peacefully. And then to get them in corrals already stuffed with other reluctant pairs. But Noah did it.

And then the ark was completed and all the cracks filled with grass and pitch. But would it float? They had done everything that God commanded. But were they careful enough?

"Keep it up," God said. "With this ark I'm going to rescue you and save all those animals to boot."

Loading the ark was a zoo! Everyone thinks a mule is stubborn. Noah and his boys had no trouble with the mules. It was the lions. They simply lay down in the dust and would not move. It was like they were not pleased with their accommodations or something. They refused to enter. They were sleepy and grumpy. The lions were left until last.

Finally the animals were loaded. Ham lost a couple toes in the process. A water buffalo's hoof caught the last two toes on his left foot. He had turned to take care of some disturbance and wasn't paying attention. But the cargo was loaded!

Of course they had no idea how they were going to close the massive door. And even if they could have, they wouldn't have wanted to. It was hot and muggy. The humidity was oppressive. Noah and his family had to wait seven days for the rain to start. At the end of that week Noah celebrated his six hundredth birthday. He felt like he was a thousand.

"My birthday present for you is my promise. I will hold you up. I will rescue you!"

Can you imagine the hecklers? For seven days, twenty-four hours a day, the townspeople gathered around the boat. Hecklers outside and nervous animals inside.

But the rains did begin to fall. In fact, it was like all the water of heaven fell down upon them. Noah was not sure how it happened, but God closed the massive door. Was it the wind or the movement of the boat as it was lifted roughly and awkwardly off the ground? Who knows? Noah was standing there one minute then a rush of water or air tipped the boat precariously to one side. When he picked himself off the floor the door was shut. Noah didn't know how God did it, but he was sure that it was God.

Noah had never been so sick in his life. He was sick in his heart because so many people were drowning outside. "When they were heckling us and threatening us with sabotage, I almost looked forward to the day when they would get theirs," Noah recounted to his boys aboard ship. But now that day had come. He wasn't the least bit happy. His heart was sick and he wept.

"I am saving you for a purpose," Noah heard God say amidst his dream.

Noah was physically sick, too. "As I wasn't skilled enough to be a shipbuilder or knowledgeable enough to be a zoologist, neither am I fit enough to be a sea captain," Noah groaned to his wife. Ugh! Those first weeks. And the storm. Noah honestly believed that God had played a cruel joke on them. He had saved them on land to watch them sink at sea.

The Wind...

And then the calm. This was the nightmare that he fought to avoid at all cost. Noah forced his tired eyes open at dawn on day one hundred and fifty. Something was different. There was a breeze. No, it was a wind. Noah rushed to find an opening, a place to drink in the wind. In spite of himself, Noah danced, first alone and then with his bedraggled wife. As the wind rushed through Noah's hair it seemed to speak the words that he had heard in his dream, the words God had spoken so long ago. "You and your family I will rescue." But what the dream lacked, the wind added. "I have not forgotten you. I am saving you right now!"

Noah's smile and change of demeanor interpreted the words of the wind to the rest of his family; yes, even to the animals. And although the waters receded gradually, time didn't matter any more. The vision that had been planted in Noah's heart so long ago had been watered by the dream. But the wind, the very breath of God, had brought life.

With a Sacrifice in Mind

Genesis 7:1-8:22

hen God was issuing the ship's manifest for the goods he wished transported safely through the destructive storm to Mount Ararat, he did so with a sacrifice in mind. Notice the manifest: 8 humans, 2 animals, male and female of every wild, domestic and creeping thing upon the earth, 7 pairs of clean animals (see the addendum to the manifest explaining the meaning of "clean" in Leviticus 11) and 7 pairs of every bird.

At the end of the voyage Noah sent forth the raven. He apparently did not make it back to the ship. "Lost at sea," was recorded in the ship's log. At seven-day intervals after that Noah released a dove. The first returned empty-beaked. The second returned bearing an olive branch, a symbol of peace to this day. The third dove did not return; presumably she found life so good on the outside that she could not bear the thought of being cooped up again.

But why did the manifest call for seven pairs of clean animals and seven pairs of every bird of the air? One submerged raven and one absent dove do not provide the answer. The answer is found in the actions of Noah after he descended from the S.S. Deliverance. Noah

set about to build an altar. He took every clean animal and every clean bird (presumably he withheld a pair of each so they could be fruitful and multiply) and offered them upon the altar as a burnt offering. We are not told if he had trouble starting the fire. Was there plenty of driftwood around? We are not told any of the details except this. The Lord was pleased by the sacrificial odor. Noah's obedience, attention for detail, and seeking heart called for the attention of God. The impact of the sacrifice reached into the very throne room of God. Then and there God vowed never to destroy the created order again.

But God was not naive. He knew the twisted nature of sin. He knew the flood was only a temporary fix to the problem of sin. Something much more extensive was needed. Notice that God himself announced, "The inclination of the human heart is evil from youth." God said that while looking at the eight crew members of the S.S. Deliverance.

When God wrote out the manifest he knew that Noah would be making a thanksgiving sacrifice at the First Temple of God on Hillside Avenue, Mount Ararat. But God also had another sacrifice in mind, a perfectly pleasing sacrifice, a sacrifice that would deal with the root of man's evil, man's inclination to sin. Sitting in the shipping office dictating the manifest to the clerk and captain of the Deliverance, God's vision penetrated time. He gazed upon the sacrifice of his Son. He murmured to himself, "Well done, my good and faithful son." With a faraway look in his eyes God recited words that had not yet been penned but nonetheless were on his heart, "Christ has appeared once and for all at the end of the age to remove sin by the sacrifice of himself."*

* Hebrews 9:26

Farid Fadel

Beware of Ravens Bearing Olive Branches

Genesis 8:1-14

he storm broke. The weather cleared. The tops of the mountains erupted through the surface of the waters like a new tooth in a child's gum. The ark scraped to a halt on a granite outcropping.

All the passengers, man and animal alike, breathed a sigh of relief. God had remembered. The monotonous ride across the surface of the seas had ended.

Noah grabbed a saw and set about the task of making an opening, a window, in the thick cypress walls. Next he went up and checked the rafters for a likely candidate, a bird strong enough to fly out over the face of the waters to survey the situation. The bird was to return and somehow the bird was to share its findings. How the bird was to do this, Noah himself hadn't figured that out.

The bird Noah chose was an aggressive, black raven. Noah grasped the powerful bird to his chest and walked toward the opening he had made. The fire of independence burned in the bird's eyes. When Noah unlatched the window and the sunlight burst into the room, the bird battled his way toward the opening. Noah sustained several painful slashes from the bird's claws. With an almost haughty crowing sound the bird soared into the light. The glaring sunlight and the sparkling water combined to make it impossible for Noah to follow the flight of the bird. The raven was gone. The raven flew back and forth across the waters. He landed for brief moments upon the rock piles but he didn't return to the boat. The raven was accustomed to the barren places. He was at home in desolation.

Noah was forced to change his strategy. He went again to the rafters of the ark. This time he spotted a small white dove. The smaller size of the bird made Noah skeptical. Noah was concerned whether the bird was up to the rigors of the world outside. But the innocence and vulnerability of this bird affected him. With each coo the bird seemed to be saying, "Try me. Try me." Noah reached for the gentle dove. It hesitated. Noah thought at first that the bird was afraid. But he quickly realized that it was not fear at all. The bird was waiting, as if asking permission to fly. At that moment Noah raised his arms and spoke lovingly to the dove, "Fly, little one, fly." The bird took to the air.

After a few hours the bird returned exhausted. Noah was waiting for her by the open window. He took the tired bird in. Obviously she had found no suitable resting place.

Seven days later, at early morning's light, Noah sent the dove out again. And, as before, Noah stood by the window. Hours passed. The hours extended long past midday. As the sun plunged toward the horizon the dove returned. A green olive branch was in her beak. Noah was elated. After the bird was returned to the eaves, Noah and his family celebrated. The white dove had returned with a green branch, an olive branch. An olive branch! The implications were not lost on Noah and his family. They danced with delight. God was in the process of providing a most necessary commodity, olives and the multi-purpose olive oil.

Seven days later the dove took flight again from the bridge of the ark. She never returned. This signaled to Noah that it was now time to remove the cover of the ark (no minor task) and eyeball the situation for himself. Yet, with top removed, Noah obediently awaited God's disembarking instructions. These came some eight weeks later.

While Noah waited on the ark, he thought about the raven and the dove. The raven was the natural for the assignment, powerful and aggressive. The dove, less powerful and gentler, was not the likely choice. The raven was willing to settle for second-best in his rush for freedom. He found what he was looking for in the desolate rocky places.

The white dove, on the other hand, had worked for the good of the floating community. The dove was very selective. She was looking for a garden-like world. And she, too, found what she was looking for.

What if the independent raven had returned with the olive branch? This would have been the ultimate in mixed messages. A devilishly dark, powerful, aggressive raven bearing an olive branch? No way! The olive branch is a symbol of peace.

Often today it is the aggressor that calls out "Peace, peace!" He carries an olive branch in one claw and a big stick in the other. Beware of ravens bearing olive branches!

Who are the people and nations who will abide under God's blessings? The spotless, the vulnerable, the gentle, the dove-like. Welcome these! God does. "Blessed are the peacemakers for they shall be called the children of God."*

*Matthew 5:9

Worship and Religious Practice

Genesis 8:20-22

*O*ne big building, preferably with stained glass, and massive oak pews.

Two scripture passages, an Old and New Testament portion, read with great respect and solemnity.

A three-point sermon, twenty minutes in length, not more than twenty-five.

A four-fold Amen by a crimson-robed choir.

One building + Two scripture passages + Three-point sermon + Four-fold Amen = A worship event that scores a ten. When such worship events take place lights flash in heaven, buzzers go off, bells ring, angels rejoice, the Elders prostrate themselves, the crystal sea foams in delight, harps begin to play celestial music, heavenly incense gives off an even more beautiful aroma . . . and God smiles. Right?

Can worship be narrowed to such a simplistic formula? The worship found in the beginning story of Genesis depicts worship in a wholly different light. Ultimately, acceptable worship revolves around an acceptance of and response to God's unmerited favor.

Worship begins with God's action. He spoke. He created. He flung. He called forth. He breathed. He finished. He longed for fellowship with his creation. He bestowed grace.

True worship is Adam and Eve before their stumble, walking in the garden with their Creator. The idea must have carried on past the fall because both Enoch and Noah's worship was described as "walking with God."

Authentic worship is Noah and his family leaving the ark after a long harrowing journey and praising the Lord. Noah built an altar and laid a sacrifice and lit a fire. The Lord smelled the odor of roasting fowl and was moved to announce that he would never again let the emotion of anger flood his heart and wipe out his creation. But was Noah's real act of worship the sacrifice of a few birds or the sacrifice of his life into the redemptive design of God? God called and Noah responded in obedience. God saved and Noah responded with thankfulness. Obedience and thankfulness are signs of worship as much as the rainbow is a sign of God's promise.

Worship is the response of awe in the presence of the Almighty. Worship is a spontaneous gratitude, not forced, not coerced. Worship is praising God for and with the breath of life that he has whistled into our souls.

Now, religious practice — that is something totally different. That speaks of offerings (acceptable and unacceptable), invoking the name of the Lord, and massive building projects to impress God and man.

Religious practice by itself is worthless and ineffectual to us. It carries no weight. It impresses us but God is totally unmoved. It is not a genuine response to the grace of God. Such practice alone is offensive to God, if not downright laughable, puny attempts to placate.

Religious practice must be connected to true worship which has its foundation in the grace of God. Like the flowering crocus is connected to the stem and the stem is rooted in the soil of God's grace, so must our worship be. Hand clapping, chorus singing, at-the-altar bending, offering giving, believer baptizing, feet washing, communion taking... yes, even sanctuary building, two-time Scripture reading, three-point sermonizing and four-fold amen-ing; all religious practice must be the blossom of our heart's desire to worship the Creator, Redeemer and Sustainer of life. All authentic worship comes from God and returns to him.

As Long as the Earth Endures

Genesis 8:20-22

he earth was at a seasonal juncture. Daily the sun warmed the air and thawed the ground. By mid-afternoon the road off the highway and onto the farmer's property was a quagmire. At sunset the puddles began to congeal, to solidify. It was simple. No sun, no heat. No heat and the thawing reversed. The cold, blustery wind blew again declaring to all that dared venture out that the battle was not finished. The icy grip of winter had not relaxed. It was as if all day winter laughed at the spring because he knew come nightfall the deep chill would return and territory that had been ceded to the advance of warmth would be reclaimed. The winter's wind let loose with a sarcastic laugh. And the earth shivered.

As the farmer bounced and spun up the road to his home he thought maybe it was time to bring in a few more truck loads of gravel to spread over his pot-holed excuse for a road. The ruts, which multiplied in direct proportion to the number of times he slipped and fishtailed his way on and off his property, had become collection points for the runoff of melting snow. Muddy puddles were everywhere. Yet the farmer whistled. He smiled. He tapped his steering wheel in time to a country-western tune. He gave the neck of his big hunting dog an affectionate hug.

The farmer put on his insulated boots and trudged out into the cold February afternoon. The wind licked at his ungloved hands. Involuntarily he blew on them. He crunched through the partially thickened ice patches that grew in the ruts. He pulled the collar up on his

coat, all the while trying to pull his longish neck down inside. He was off to check the supplies. The forecaster was saying that winter might hang on longer this year. The farmer wanted to make sure that his few stock animals would have enough feed.

A snowball flew by and just ticked the end of his frozen ear. Pain! As he turned he saw his high school-aged son ready for battle. In the midst of the cold, in the midst of the wind, in the midst of the mud, father and son engaged in a brief free-for-all. Laughter could be heard across the farm. After ten minutes of fast and furious snowballing, father and son collapsed in a heap on some hay bales near the barn. They looked like two steam engines, older and newer, side-by-side, panting after a long, hard pull. Sweat dripped off the father's brow, down his neck and under his collar.

Farmer and future farmer went together to check the supplies. Then they stopped in the well-insulated metal barn where the expensive and highly-efficient farm machinery was kept. The father had been spending more and more time in this place. Every piece of equipment was ready, every joint well oiled, every spark plug cleaned, every engine tuned. The farmer was eager to get into his fields to begin planting.

And his seeds were purchased and ready. Bank loans had been secured long ago against the success of this very crop. The fields had already been designated for rotation, some for soybeans and others for corn. Father and son planned the strategy.

Yet outside the wind shrieked. It looked for any opening it could find in the metal building as if it felt it were somehow being left out of a very important meeting. The ice formed again in the ruts. A snow flurry blew in from the north. People rushed to plug in their diesel engines. The temperature dropped. A storm approached.

Father and son emerged from the barn and headed for the warmth of the kitchen. On the enclosed porch they removed their muddy boots and clothes.

Dinner was on the table. Fried chicken, mashed potatoes, gravy, cole slaw and hot biscuits. A cherry pie sat on the sideboard.

Well-satisfied after dinner, mother, father and son sat around the piles of chicken bones, crusty plates and empty milk glasses and had devotions. The father read from Genesis 8. They had been reading and discussing their way through Genesis. It had taken them more than three weeks to get this far, not because they were inconsistent in their

devotions but because they enjoyed the family activity so much. And the father read:

As long as the earth endures, seedtime and harvest, cold and heat, summer and winter, day and night shall not cease.

Father and son looked at each other and a smile passed between them. They knew why they enjoyed this time of winter. Spring was just around the corner. And with spring came planting. And with planting came harvest.

God was dependable. He could be trusted. In the midst of the darkness of night and the blow of winter, God was bringing daylight and springtime. It was so. God had said it and they had experienced it in the past.

Down the Plank Came the Hunters

Genesis 9:1-12

The floodwaters were forced into their designated areas by the breath of God. Dry land appeared. At the command of God Noah released the anxious animals into their new habitat. And down the plank came the hunters.

In the innocence of the garden, falcon and sparrow flew together in tight formation. The wolf and the lamb frolicked as friends. The ox and the lion were both vegetarians. But that was so long ago. It seemed that time had simply flooded by, and indeed it had.

What was it that changed these harmonious garden-dwellers into a society with a distinct pecking order? Animals that we declare "natural enemies" were not always like that. Why the change? Perhaps it was the long boat ride together in close quarters. Perhaps there was jealousy because of the cabin assignments. Perhaps some animals felt slighted at chow time. Perhaps the rhino was always horning in. The beaver was too destructive. The tiger too noisy. The pig too messy. The horsefly too annoying.

Whatever we imagine, the picture is this. When the animals walked up the plank they were creatures that instinctively cared for and looked out for one another.

97

Hunting License

This card allows the bearer to hunt or trap anything that moves. The purpose of hunting is for food. This does not authorize hunting for sport.

Lifetime Validity

Authorized Signature

God

But when they waddled, soared, hopped, thundered, slithered, padded, darted, and ambled down the plank they did so as hunters and the hunted.

Maybe their order down the plank had something to do with it. The beetle went first. His slow pace made him a natural target for the wolf spider. The spider, still licking his chops after a beetle buffet, was accosted by the scorpion. The scorpion made quick work of the spider with his two front claws and deadly stinger. Up at the top of the plank a grasshopper mouse witnessed the whole drama. He was hungry after the long voyage and ready for action. So he darted quickly down the ramp and bit off the stinger of the scorpion. Then the mouse was free to dine on the scorpion. Satisfied with his supper, the mouse headed off to rest in the crevice of a large rock. He never made it for floating above on the wind currents was an owl. With blinding speed the owl swooped down, and in a flash of feathers the mouse was history.

Well, maybe this didn't happen right off the boat. Maybe the animals took some time to be fruitful and multiply before they developed such violent traits. What is obvious is that down the plank came the hunters.

And what about man? He, too, came down the plank a hunter. God gathered Noah and his sons at the top of the gangplank and issued four hunting licenses. He announced that hunting season was now open. The laminated cards had a picture of the hunter on the front. In big print under the picture it read:

HUNTING LICENSE

This card allows the bearer to hunt or trap anything that moves. The purpose of hunting is for food. This card does not authorize hunting for sport.

Lifetime validity.   Authorizing Signature
                                              GOD

This side of the card was stamped with the seal of God's Fish and Game Department. The seal was a rainbow with a lake trout jumping at one end and an elk grazing at the other. A mallard flew among the bands of color. The card had no expiration date. It was valid until the bearer died.

On the reverse side of the card there were two notifications. The first stated that all animals hunted or trapped must have the blood removed before they could be consumed. The second, more important than the first, was written in all capital letters. It read:

**THIS LICENSE IS NOT VALID FOR
THE HUNTING OR TRAPPING OF
HUMANS. SUCH HUNTING IS
STRICTLY FORBIDDEN. VIOLATORS
WILL BE SEVERELY PUNISHED.**

When the animals descended the plank out of the ark they did so as hunters and the hunted. When man descended, he left with a hunting license in his pocket. The great distinction between animal and man was not the card. The great distinction was that man was never to be hunted, trapped or killed by another man. The reason was simple. God had explained it at the top of the plank as he handed out the licenses. "You are made in my image."

Whoever Sheds the Blood of Man

Genesis 9:5-6

*T*he steel doors squealed as they slid open. The guards entered James Wilmore's cell. The prisoner was headed for sentencing.

Not long ago James had taken the life of an elderly man. It had all started as a simple break-in. James thought no one was home. "In and out," he said to himself with a smile. First the living room. A quick glance around. Nothing that he could carry out in a rush. He was looking for quick turnover items or, even better, cash.

He quietly stalked down the hallway in the dark. As often as he had done this he never felt safe until he was out of the house and blocks away. His heart pounded in his ears as the adrenaline pumped through his system. This adrenaline was almost addictive. For James the thrill of breaking and entering was never gone until he came face-to-face with the owner of the house and his handgun.

James reacted instinctively. In the struggle the elderly man was shot. As he lay dead in a crimson pool, James fled. On the way out James spotted a cassette recorder, some cash, and some other small items in the bedroom. Snatching them, he fled. Once out on the street and ten minutes away from the scene of the murder, James tried to calm himself down. But he couldn't. Never before had he killed anyone. He always fashioned himself as a hero thief, a Robin Hood of sorts. He didn't rob people to feed a growing drug habit or to amass great wealth. He committed his crimes to kind of get back at the system that he believed had enslaved his family, taken away his dignity, and destroyed his future.

Twenty-nine year old James was a generous crook. Much of the take of his crimes was given to children and the homeless in the area. And that was how he was caught. A small boy in the apartment block next to his own was ill. James gave the cassette recorder to the boy's mother thinking the boy would be comforted by the music. The mother, in need of money to buy medicine, pawned the recorder.

The police discovered the cassette player on a routine visit to the pawnshop. It was identified because the elderly man was a meticulous record keeper. He had inventoried his entire house, serial numbers and all. The trail led back to the mother, and through the mother, to James. James was arrested and charged with murder.

The trial by jury was really uneventful. James pleaded guilty. He was assured by his court-appointed lawyer that he would get off with a fairly light sentence; after all, he had never killed anyone before. "And besides," the lawyer intoned, "our jails are very crowded. We simply can't afford to keep you in jail for an extended period of time."

The courtroom was rather empty. Only a few friends of James bothered to show. The elderly man who had been killed had no known family members. Still, there was a smattering of conversation in the courtroom. It was silenced by the words of the bailiff, "All rise."

Judge Richardson strode purposefully into the room. He climbed the three steps that placed him at a higher level than anyone else in the room. By virtue of his level above the court he commanded respect. His black robe and graying temples added an air of dignity.

Judge Richardson had served on the bench for a number of years. He had presided over many cases such as this, some that were exponentially more gruesome than this one. The judge had developed a reputation for fairness. He was even-handed with attorneys and their clients alike.

It was common knowledge that Richardson was a Christian. He was active in his church, serving on the Elder's Board. Over the past month

Judge Richardson's pastor had been leading his congregation through a Bible study. Again and again the pastor had called his people to faithfully apply God's Word in the workplace. The judge had signed a covenant with other members in his congregation that read, in part:

"Believing that God's Word is a true and reliable source of wisdom, faith, practice and encouragement for today, I, _____, will actively look for opportunities to appropriately and faithfully apply the Bible in my daily life."

After the preliminaries, Judge Richardson announced that the time of sentencing was at hand. "Would the defendant please rise?" he asked. James Wilmore stood with his lawyer.

Judge Richardson read the charges against James Wilmore. "James Wilmore, you have been found guilty of first-degree murder by a jury of your peers." The judge paused and then pulled a typewritten sheet from a black folder on his desk. Did he know that what he was about to do would send shock waves through the legal and religious communities, first on the West Coast and then across the rest of the United States? Most, in retrospect, believe that he did.

The judge read: "From each man, I, God, will demand an accounting for the life of his fellow man. Whoever sheds the blood of man, by man shall his blood be shed; for in the image of God have I, God, made him."

Silence was like a vacuum in the courtroom. Animation returned as the ramifications of Judge Richardson's words sank in. The judge continued, "On the basis of the evidence before this court and on the basis of the Word of God, the holy standard upon which this country was founded, I sentence you, James Wilmore, to hang by a rope until you are dead."

The defendant sat stunned. He had been promised a relatively light sentence. Instead, he was sentenced to the extreme extent of the law. The defense attorney was outraged. He muttered to himself, "I have never heard of such a thing." He called for a retrial. He assured his client that he would appeal. The judge sat unmoved. Outside there was no visible evidence of the turmoil that raged within. Inside he was churning with conflicting emotions.

A local news reporter, Bernard Michaels, covered the courthouse scene. He just happened to be in Judge Richardson's courtroom at the time of sentencing. Michaels had stuck his head in at various times throughout the trial and had predetermined that there was no story of note taking place. Now he knew he had been wrong - very wrong.

The story appeared in the Sun Times the next morning. "Judge Throws the Book (the Bible) at Convicted Murderer". It was necessary for the judge to get an unlisted number. He received hate mail. His life was threatened. He was charged with incompetence. Whispers of "Whoever thought of sentencing a man to death based on some old story in the Bible?" could be heard in the courthouse. Even people in his own congregation turned on him.

All reactions were not negative. Many Bible-believers praised the judge. They were encouraged. Christians from many walks of life seriously considered how they could faithfully apply God's Holy Word in their daily lives. Holiness and faithfulness among Christians increased.

Of course the television magazine shows were quick to capitalize on the sensational story. It became the hot topic of the day. Judge Richardson decided to appear on one cable T.V. show to answer questions. Those who called in were roughly split down the middle with condemnation and commendation.

Following the interview Michaels wrote an article entitled: "Judge Sticks to His Guns on Capital Punishment". The story was picked up by both the A.P. and the U.P.I. It received a worldwide release.

The controversy raged in diners and truck stops and all the way to the floor of the Senate.

Judge Richardson resigned from the bench amid howls of derision. He returned to his private practice.

Bernard Michaels later went on to write a best-selling book about the trial and its effects on the practice of the death penalty in the United States.

And James Wilmore? He now sits on death row in the state where he committed his crime. He is in his third and final appeal.

The Inlaid Bow

Genesis 9:1-17

he bow was made of lightly stained hickory wood. The hickory had been expertly polished so that it literally shined. The grains of the wood added to both the beauty and the strength of the weapon. The bow was inlaid with precious gems - sapphires, rubies and diamonds. There were also generous additions of mother-of-pearl along the spine of the bow. There was no carving on this bow, no great scenes of the hunt. It wasn't that there was no room for such carving. It is just that the owner of the bow did not care for hunting. The owner took no pleasure in bringing down what he had intentionally and wonderfully made. Was this an instrument of destruction or just an artifact for display? Most definitely it was a weapon, an awesome weapon. In the hands of an expert this bow was lethal.

This exquisite bow sat unstrung in the corner of the master's throne room. Beside the bow rested an immense quiver of finely sharpened arrows. The feathering on the arrows was distinctive. They were made up of an assortment of blue, white and red feathers. The master always said that the coloring indicated the heavenly origin, the holy intentions and the hallowed sacrifice.

The master never used the special bow that stood unstrung in the corner. That bow was reserved for a time of the master's choosing. Neither did he fit the special arrows to the string of another, lesser bow. The bow and the arrows were a matched set, a sanctified combination. In recent days, however, the master had been practicing. At the far edge of heaven the master had set up a target. At three thousand paces he scored the target repeatedly with hair-splitting accuracy. It was an amazing thing to behold. It was perfection.

It was obvious to the entire heavenly host that the master's regret was growing. In direct correspondence to the recklessly, out-of-control spiral of sin on his well-fashioned globe, the master's righteous anger spiraled, as well. The further away man wandered from God, the further away he moved the target. Even at six thousand paces now he continued to hit the mark with every arrow.

What it was that finally moved the master off the practice range and into his throne room, not one of the heavenly host knew. The master very intentionally strode into his throne room just after sunrise and picked up the bow and the quiver. As if a charge of static electricity passed through the heavenly host, the hair on the back of the angels' necks and the hair on their arms stood erect. It was an unearthly feeling. A tingle of excitement mixed with a major dose of dread.

God marched to the edge of heaven and peered down. Resting one end of the hickory bow on the ground, the master bent the bow to the string. It took massive strength in his arms, shoulders and lower back. With no little effort the loop of the bowstring slipped into the top notch. The bow was strung. The deadly weapon prepared. From the quiver the master withdrew one arrow from among many. Lovingly he caressed the feathers. Next the groove at the feathered end of the arrow was placed on the string. The master paused. It was as if he were talking to himself, asking himself if this indeed was the radical step that he wanted to take. Convinced, he raised the bow to shoulder height and took aim. Slowly the bow was bent. The arc increased. As the master increased the tension on the string the bow responded. With bow fully extended to near its breaking point, the muscular arms of the master strained beyond endurance. Yet, the master stopped. It was as if someone had chiseled an archer in stone.

And then with the imperceptible movement of the index and middle fingers on the master's right hand, the arrow flew, true and straight. At the snap of the bowstring lightning and thunder exploded in the air. The arrow seemed to tear through the heavenlies and ripped open clouds that were pregnant with water. Inundating water flooded toward earth. The earth became a cup full to overflowing. And yet the arrow tore on. More and more clouds were slashed with the expertly honed edge of the well-chosen arrow from God's quiver. And the waters poured down, the destructive and cleansing waters poured down. Forty days the waters poured down.

And for many more than forty days the master stood at the edge of heaven, bow still in hand, but now in a resting position, as if he were a child who had thrown a piece of bark into a raging current and was trying to watch where it would wash up. The master's piece of bark was an ark. On that ark he rested his entire redemptive plans.

When the time was complete the waters receded and the ark drifted ashore. A tiny remnant of people and animals exited the ark. The people made an altar and offered a pleasing sacrifice. It was the odor of that sacrifice that roused the master to action. With one giant step the master moved from heaven to earth. In the presence of the master the people bowed in silent reverence.

It was the master who spoke. He placed his hand of blessing on the heads of the few. The same hand that had created the world. The same hand that had fashioned the bow. The same hand that had bent the bow and shot forth the arrow. With that same powerful right hand the master blessed his creation.

And then the master did an utterly astounding thing. With a great cry of pent-up emotion he flung the bow skyward. The bow defied gravity and remained in the heavens. "This is a sign of the covenant that I make between me and you and every living creature that is with you, for all future generations: I have set my bow in the clouds, and it shall be a sign of the covenant between me and you and every living creature of all flesh; and the waters shall never again become a flood to destroy all flesh."

That finely crafted, specially inlaid bow became a symbol in the heavens of the master's eternal promise to seek another solution to the wretched problem of human sinfulness. And today after a storm the sapphires, rubies, diamonds and mother-of-pearl inlaid in that bow sparkle to remind us that we worship a master who is faithful to his promise.

The Rev. Dr. Noah

Genesis 9:20-24

oah found favor in the sight of the Lord. Noah walked with God. Noah pleased God. Noah spoke with God. Noah was obedient to God. Noah was the vessel that God used to save mankind and all creation from total annihilation. Noah was obviously one in a million. Noah, plain and simple, was a good ole' boy in God's book. Noah was the man's man of faith. He is listed right up there in the Hebrews' Hall of Fame. Copies of the now-yellowed, water-stained photo of Noah with a rainbow-draped ark in the background hangs proudly in any children's Bible. The citation below the picture reads: "Because Noah had faith, he was warned about something that had not yet happened. He obeyed and built a boat that saved him and his family. In this way the people of the world were judged, and Noah was given the blessings that come to everyone who pleases God."

Noah would have made an excellent pastor. Eager for communion with God. Self-sacrificing. Jack-of-all-trades. Ecology-minded. Prophetic. Pastoral. In tune with the Spirit of God. Authoritative, in a godly sort of way. Amazing worship leader. A man on whom the very blessing of God rested. A man who had experienced the rough times and had lived to tell about them, by God's grace. One who saw signs of hope coming in the clouds.

What potential! Granted, it would have been a little hard for Noah to gather around him a mega-church when all the non-churched Joes and Marys had been recently washed away. Nonetheless, you can just imagine Rev. Dr. Noah reading the Scripture like he had lived it, praying like he conversed daily with the Redeemer, preaching like he had seen first-hand the ravages of sin and God's powerful hand of judgment, altar-calling like one who knew about grace close up and personal, and granting blessings like he himself had been blessed.

If your church was looking for a pastor to lead you into the twenty-first century, no doubt if you could find a man with half the leadership qualities, experience and grace of Noah, you would snatch him right up.

With all these glorious things to say about Noah, it's a shame that the closing picture we have of Brother Noah is as a drunken, naked curser of his children. Noah sets out vividly the dangers of pastoral ministry. Busy saving the world but neglecting his own family. Blessing everyone else's children but cursing his own.

What an immense contrast: God's gracious unconditional blessings side-by-side with Pastor Noah's damning and cursing. God's faithfulness side-by-side with Dr. Noah's foolishness and fickleness. God's expansive call to humankind side-by-side with Rev. Noah's narrow-minded bigotry.

Rev. Dr. Noah was a great man of faith. He did great things for God. But he forgot one very important lesson. "Be careful not to curse that which God has blessed."

God has blessed the family . . . yours included.

Dr. Simon Serpentine, Speech Therapist

Genesis 10:1-11:9

*J*epheth was a stutterer. In the norm he was able to make himself understood, but even Noah had trouble figuring out everything that his son was saying. Ssssometimes it wawawas just very hahahard to fififgure out what hehehe wanted to sasasay. All of Jepheth's descendants grew up in their land, in their clan groupings, forming their nations. They all grew up ssspeaking the sasasame way.

Ham had a lisp. He, too, had trouble making himself understood. Noah became very adept at understanding Ham. Thumtimeth it wath ethpathally hard to underthand him. All of Ham's descendants grew up in their land, in their clan groupings, forming their nations. They all grew up theaking the thame way.

Shem cut off the ends of his words. If people carefully tuned in they could grasp Shem's message, but it was not without a great deal of effort. Sometim it wa especial har to understan him. All of Shem's descendants grew up in their land, in their clan groupings, forming their nations. The all gre up spea the sa wa.

No one is sure what caused the great migration from the east. Some believe it was a drought. Others believe that there was a sign of sorts in the sky. Yet others believed there was a great volcano. Whatever the cause, the fact remains that a migration of immense proportions took place.

As the families of Japheth, Ham and Shem moved toward the plain of Shinar, stuttering, lisping, and word-chopping could be heard among the various wagons. As long as the groups remained separated, problems were few. When they came together, however, to graze their animals, to obtain water from limited sources, or to settle disputes, confusion reigned.

Enter Dr. Simon Serpentine. He was a self-appointed doctor. He was a quack, really. Painted on the side of his canvas wagon cover were the words:

DR. SIMON SERPENTINE
SPEECH THERAPIST

"Dr. Simon," as the people began to call him, made a big impression on the various tribes. He knew just what to do to help each group of people speak clearly and properly. At first he had classes with individual clan leaders. He convinced them of the value of his services. Then once he had the blessing of the clan heads, he took a handful from each people group and trained them. Once he had educated the stutterer, the lisper and the word-chopper, he called his students together for a conference. It was open to all those who were migrating.

It was something to behold. In the center of a vast circle were twelve persons. At first the twelve were rather shy. But, with encouragement from Dr. Simon, they began to speak.

Dr. Simon Serpentine had predetermined the discussion topic. "What could we do if we all spoke the same language?"

In the end, the forum was like a great harvest for Dr. Simon Serpentine. People were convinced of his vital role within the gathered community. Also, the people jointly and individually decided that if they pulled together they could do some truly monumental things.

Through his twelve trained teachers, Dr. Serpentine was able to shape the thoughts and desires of the plain dwellers.

One day Dr. Serpentine introduced a new topic. "How could we, the community gathered on the plain, really make a name for ourselves?" The ideas flew fast and furious. He was content in the knowledge that he had turned the people's thoughts away from God toward themselves.

With great enthusiasm the people began to work. They couldn't believe how easy it was to work together now that they all spoke the same language, used the same vocabulary and utilized the same accent and same pronunciation. Work progressed quickly.

When the building was completed Dr. Simon Serpentine whispered into the ears of a few of his teachers, "Don't you think it would be a good idea to dedicate this building in honor of the one who made this all possible?" The idea was an instant hit.

The dedication service was set for 6 p.m. a week to the day following the completion of the marvelous building. The building was really a sight to behold. The top of the building reached the heavens. The base was broad and well established. Leaders from all the clans were invited to speak. The honored guest was Dr. Simon Serpentine himself.

Following windy speeches about the community spirit which enabled the project to reach completion and boring monologues about the technical wizardry of the building itself, the focus of the meeting turned toward Dr. Simon Serpentine. Dr. Simon sat on the platform in his three-piece polyester suit with reversible vest. A small rosebud was pinned to his lapel. He was beaming a devilish brand of pride. With each remark about his invaluable service and behind-the-scenes leadership qualities, Dr. Simon's self-estimation increased. (That was a particularly amazing thing since Dr. Serpentine already thought he was on a par with God himself.)

At last the unveiling. A bronze plaque of dedication was uncovered. It read:

> "THIS TOWER OF BRICK AND MORTAR IS
> LOVINGLY DEDICATED TO DR. SIMON
> SERPENTINE. WITHOUT HIS DIRECTION
> AND INSPIRATION WE, THE PEOPLE OF
> THE PLAIN, WOULD NEVER HAVE BEEN
> ABLE TO MAKE A NAME FOR OURSELVES."

God, who had not been invited to the ceremony, grew ill. He could not bear with these sinful people a moment longer. The earth began to shake and the massive building began to crumble. People ran for their lives. In their fear the stuttering, lisping and word-chopping returned. In great panic people were not able to understand each other. Tempers flared. Cooperation ceased.

A hot dry breath blew across the plain, trash swirling. Nothing remained on the plain except the trash and a mound of blackened mud bricks. It was obvious that the garbage and the mud bricks would be covered by the encroaching sand in a matter of weeks.

The people were scattered. Stutterers to the East. Lispers to the West. Word-choppers to the North. And a new group of people, an immense lot, really, went South. These persons were deaf and dumb. Dr. Simon Serpentine stood on the platform looking out over the vast emptiness. The people, in their haste to clear out, left Dr. Simon's specially crafted textbooks and teaching aids on the floor of the plain.

Dr. Simon was thoroughly disgusted. He had been so close. In that moment Dr. Simon Serpentine vowed to try again. He laughed to himself. Maybe all this will work for the advancement of my kingdom. Now all the people are divided. As long as they are divided I can play one group against the other. The ideas of race hatred, Klan marches, ethnic cleansings, vigilantes, death camps and numerous other forms of man's inhumanity to man entered his fiendish mind.

The grand celebration on the Plain of Shinar had been disrupted. There could be no mistake about that. But Dr. Simon Serpentine was still involved in history. And he intended on making a big impact.

A Heart Attack, Who God?

Genesis 1-11

od slumped on the rim of the world and wondered what things would have been like if Adam and Eve would have obeyed, if Cain would have listened, if revenge hadn't reared its ugly head, if innocence wouldn't have ceased to exist, if humankind wasn't so self-seeking and self-serving, if his marvelous creation hadn't been ravaged. Pain gripped the heart of God. God was having a heart attack. He had all the symptoms: shortness of breath, tingling sensations in his arms and an intense burning in his chest.

Then God thought of Noah, the only righteous man that God could find in Noah's generation. God thought of the ark, the obedience, the animals saved, the pleasing sacrifice, the rainbow and the promise. The pain lessened. The discomfort eased. God's breathing returned to normal. God could raise his arms once more.

God lifted his feet and placed them on his footstool. He rested. More comfortable now, he looked around hoping for another like Noah in this generation. Off in the distance, barely visible to the divine eye, God saw a group of persons. With coordinated movement, as if to music, the people worked. "Working on what?" God wondered aloud. A spasm of pain entered the outer lining of God's heart. God stepped down from the rim of the earth and realized that the people had gathered to lift themselves up. It was Adam and Eve's desire to be like God, except now it was a group activity, as if combining to build a seven-story ziggurat would make them divine. God's fuse burned short. From horizon to horizon he scattered these ungrateful creatures. Peace and harmony had been replaced by hatred and discord. Wars and rumors of wars became the norm. The drumbeats of hatred and prejudice were heard throughout the earth. God doubled over in pain. His heart felt as if it were being torn in two.

"God having a heart attack? Please!" you scoff. "As if God, by virtue of the fact that he must inhale the smoke of the world, or by being too busy with deskwork to exercise, or by eating one too many French fries, has somehow damaged his heart muscle or clogged his arteries. Give me a break!"

Oh, to be sure, God, the maker and sustainer of life, is not being threatened with a triple by-pass. His existence is not in danger. He is not headed for some heavenly coronary care unit after exceeding his limits on a treadmill. Yet each act of rebellion, every murder of reputation or gangland killing, each incident of sexual promiscuity or incident of envy, lack of compassion, or lust, tears at the very heart of God. Simply put, human sin affects God.

Man's righteousness, as in the case of Noah, has a healing effect on the heart of God. True righteousness is only found in Christ. Amazing. God's massive coronary of the cross brought us righteousness. And our righteousness of being found in Christ brings healing to God's heart.

Out of the Quicksand

Genesis 11:22-32

erah was a prosperous landowner in Ur. Yet things were not like they had once been. The religious community greatly taxed Terah's land. Terah grew agitated as the local priests grew fat, powerful and wealthy off his industry. Deep within Terah's heart dissatisfaction multiplied. The stories of caravans from as far away as the land of Canaan strangely beckoned.

One dark and moonless night Terah had a dream. He saw a land flowing with milk and honey. His family was there and was prospering. He heard beautiful words of blessing, yet they were somehow indistinguishable. The dream passed. His soul had been stirred. But Terah was practical, too practical to be carried away by dreams. He was religious and dreams certainly fit into his religious belief. Yet individuals had little or no say in such matters in Ur. He knew he should go for some sort of interpretation of the dream. Even without going to the priests, Terah knew what their interpretation would be. The bottom line was that Terah was much too important to their power base. They would never let him go with their blessing, dream or no dream.

Practically, Terah was well placed within the community of Ur. His grandfather Serug and his father Nahor had labored long and hard to make the family holdings some of the most valuable in the whole valley. Besides that, perhaps as a result of that, Terah himself was well respected. Terah was one of the elders who sat by the gate to give counsel and judgment.

Terah had three sons. He needed them as much as they needed him. The father needed the sons because they were his social security, his hedge against aging. The sons needed the father because he was their entrance to places of power. Terah had connections and Abram, Nahor and Haran were greatly advanced by them.

No, Terah could not possibly consider moving out of Ur. His dream would remain just that, a dream. Resettlement was purely out of the question for practical reasons.

Also, Terah was a religious man. In spite of the fact that Terah didn't like just being a brick in the religious status quo, and he detested the priest's costly intrusion in all corners of his life, he nonetheless felt the need of someone to divine the future for him. He was especially curious about what would happen to his children, what the next harvest would bring, and what his existence would be like beyond the grave. More importantly, in a very deep and inexplicable way, Terah felt the need of some intercession with the Divine. His own sinfulness plagued him. Terah desperately wanted someone to placate a God who could easily grow malevolent. Terah wasn't about to act on his dream of resettlement for religious reasons.

In a man's life, when practical obstructions are welded to religious constraints, he becomes immobilized, incapable of following a dream. It is like trying to maintain a forward momentum and direction in the midst of quicksand, a quagmire of immense sucking power. A force greater than the suction of the quicksand is required to set the captive free. The force that extracted Terah from the quicksand of Ur was the death of his youngest son.

At one of the many religious festivals in Ur, Terah went and searched out a diviner. He wanted to ask again about the future of his sons. Each of his three sons was married but only his boy, Haran, had a child, a son named Lot. Terah had specifically asked about the futures of his sons and grandson. The old and wrinkled seer promised him that each of his sons and his grandson would live long and prosperous lives in Ur. The words "in Ur" were emphasized. Each was singled out for a few well-chosen words of blessing. The priest said that Abram and Lot's destinies were somehow melted together, but as to how and when this would all take place, the seer said he needed more time and, of course, money to be able to decipher the signs in the heavens. One of the things of special importance to Terah that the old man predicted was this: Abram and Sari would have children that would outnumber the very sands of the vast desert to the west. Now that was significant! Terah laughed to himself at the obvious exaggeration of the seer. So many children? Yet, it was like music to Terah's ears that Abram and Sari would have children. They had been married eight years now and were still childless. Terah was delighted.

Terah tipped the seer generously and rushed off to speak with his offspring about their futures. "What were the words the diviner had said?" he thought as he hurried through the dusty streets. "'Long and prosperous lives in Ur,' – yes, that is what he had prophesied. I guess my dreams about Canaan were nonsense." A smile of settled contentment broke across the face of Terah. "We will stay in Ur and make our home here forever..." Terah's happy thoughts were shattered as he neared the gate to his home. Wailing, intense wailing, assailed his ears. It was the sound of death. Terah knew the sound very well. "But who? And why coming from my house? Surely there has been some mistake."

There was no mistake. The sound was escaping from family members and servants, his family members and his servants. The only question that remained was "Who?" Terah entered the world where everything happens in slow motion.

When and how Terah had entered his home, he did not know. As Terah woke from the daze, he was face-to-face with Abram and Nahor. They were dressed in mourning clothes. Abram was speaking, " . . . and that's where we found him. He had obviously been robbed. Haran is dead. Apparently he never had a chance." Terah stared in disbelief. What about the words of blessing? "Long prosperous lives in Ur." The words mocked Terah now. In that moment of grief-filled reasoning Terah decided what he would do. As soon as they could leave Ur they would do so. Everything that could not be carried would be sold. Family, friends and neighbors came to try to speak to Terah, to talk him out of this foolishness. When the priest came by, the seer who had spoken with such promise about his family's future, Terah did an unheard-of thing. He refused to see the holy man.

In a matter of weeks Terah, Abram, Sari and Lot bid farewell to Nahor and his wife, Milcah. Nahor had decided to stay in Ur. He was convinced that his future lay in that city. Terah argued but Nahor remained firm. Nahor felt that Terah was acting rashly in the midst of his grief. Nahor lashed out at Abram for encouraging the old man. Abram remained quiet in the face of the criticism. Abram was the oldest. It was his duty to go. In the end the three men came to an agreement of sorts. The yelling and fighting passed as the day of departure approached. The realization dawned on all three that this would likely be the last time they would be together in this life. Each wept bitterly the morning of separation.

Terah and his caravan went northwest up the Euphrates river valley.

It was a hard journey for all, but especially for Terah. He never complained, never whined, never looked back. Never again would the quicksand of practicality and religious observance hinder Terah from his dream.

In spite of his fatigue, around the fire under the twinkling heavens, Terah shared his dream with Abram and Lot. The dream was like good seed planted in the rich soil. Abram and Lot grew enthusiastic, in a subdued sort of way, about Terah's dream. It was becoming their dream as well.

By the time the travelers reached the city of Haran, Terah looked like a worn piece of leather. It was obvious to all that he would never be able to make the trip south into Canaan. Abram took charge. "We will settle down here," he commanded. The family looked for land, made a good purchase and took root in the community.

On his deathbed Terah spoke to Abram alone. "My son," he spoke, so weakly that Abram had to bend over his father's mouth to hear, "as we traveled to this place I told you of my dream. Don't let the dream die." He made Abram promise. With his last dregs of energy Terah spoke of the diviner's words about many children and his divinely appointed connection with Lot. That the seer had been mistaken about one part of the prophecy did not seem to deter Terah's faith in the remaining prophecy.

Later Terah called Abram and Lot in one final time. "Do not stay in Haran," he ordered. I will not have my family live in this place. To me it speaks of death. Haran, your brother, died in spite of the empty promises of the priests. Now I will die in this place. God forbid that anyone else among our family die in this wretched city." Terah died reciting the dream of Canaan.

Conclusion: "Rescued Through the Mirror"

inoculars and bird books, hair spray and rollers, a dining fly and extra blankets had all been set aside. The family was in their final shakedown before they began their wilderness trek. Canned foods were replaced with dehydrated ones. A large cooking pot was replaced with a smaller, more manageable one. Collapsible jugs were substituted for a hard plastic jerry can. Bathroom supplies were cut down to the basics: tooth brushes, tooth paste, soap, wash cloths and towels, a comb and brush, and, of course, toilet paper. Mom decided that she could live with Dad for a few days if he went without shaving so the shaving cream and razor were removed. Brother decided he could do without his CD player. Sister conceded that her romance novels could stay. Dad agreed that his fishing gear need not make the trip, even though he had heard great stories of the large trout that populated the streams along the trail. The family gave in and let him carry a collapsible rod but under one condition. "You carry it!" they said in unison.

Surprisingly the item that caused the biggest commotion in the whole shakedown procedure was the camera. Mom and Dad both lobbied hard for the camera. They felt that it was necessary in order to record the trip for the family history. "After all," they argued, "someday you may want to tell your kids about this trip. You'll want to have some pictures to show, won't you?" The whole issue of photography was a bit troublesome because both kids had been begging their parents to buy a digital camera, "something that we could easily carry in our pocket." With lack of funds cited for the hundredth time as the reason to refrain from such a purchase, the old bulky Nikon was included. Dad realized very quickly that he would have to carry it.

120

Over the Thanksgiving weekend the family loaded the aging (Dad called it "vintage") Volkswagen van and drove out of town, up into the mountains, toward the trailhead. They didn't bother checking in at the ranger station.

With four brightly colored and bulky backpacks, the family started down the well-worn path. Just before starting, Dad set the camera on a fence post (the tripod had been jettisoned in the shakedown as well), engaged the automatic timer and rushed to join the picture. The photo would later reveal clean clothes, polished boots, freshly shaven faces, well-combed hair, happy smiles, and eager anticipation. Out of the corner of Dad's shirt a map could be seen. All was visible in the picture.

From the beginning the trail meandered in a southeasterly direction. The trail weaved its way through a pine forest. The cool air and the pine scent made an invigorating aroma. It was wonderful indeed. Several times the four commented on how clean and refreshing the air was. "Tonic for the soul," Dad intoned. They all enjoyed the beauty of the created order around them.

The sister made a few sketches of the colorings of several birds. She wanted to look them up in the Audubon book that she had left behind. She was a real bird lover. "Imagine how much fun God must have had dreaming up all this variety!" she said to no one in particular. She privately wished that she had made a better case for bringing the binoculars along.

The second day of their hike took the family by some rugged rock formations. The father checked his map and determined that if they hiked west for roughly a day, they would again strike the trail they were on as it looped toward its beginning. Common sense and the map itself warned that they should stay on the clearly marked trail. Not being the adventuresome type, the mother was not particularly keen about leaving the footpath. "We really should stay on the marked trail," she said. "Doesn't the map warn us about the dangers of heading off on our own?" she fretted. Father responded, "You know, honey, we spend our lives living according to the suggestions and advice of others. I am really tired of 'shoulds' and 'oughts'." Brother chimed in, "Yeah, Mom, let's have some fun. Let's break a few rules for once. Lighten up." Mother winced a bit at the part of breaking the rules. Sister did not. She was nodding her head enthusiastically. "Come on, Mom. Let's go for it." The mother caved in to the insistence of the other three. So, in a moment that could be called "rebellion," all four family members agreed to disregard the map's warnings and strike out on their own. The trail, although beautiful, had become routine. The four longed for adventure. Before leaving the trail they took another picture. Rather large rock formations could be seen in the background. Snow clouds were positioned just above the rocks.

The place where they decided to set up camp for the night was by one of those trout-filled streams. Dad, without his customary waders, tried to perch on a rock in the center of the stream. Fly rod in hand he set about casting. In moments he had a bite. He called to his daughter on shore, "Get the camera. I've got a big one here!" She was already prepared. But she wasn't waiting for a picture of the fish. She was waiting for what happened next. In his excitement about landing the "big one" the father took a misstep. Down he went. Splash! The daughter was a little slow with the shutter so she missed the actual fall. What she was able to record was the result, her father seated in ice-cold water, a grimace on his face. They all grimaced when they discovered that their map was ruined.

A hot supper of dehydrated noodles and beans helped them all feel better. They weren't able to supplement the meal with trout. But that was okay. They laughed all the way to bed. Snow fell that night and temperatures plummeted.

They wouldn't have laughed so hard if they knew what was going to happen to one of their brightly colored packs. A bear came around that evening to check out the new arrivals in his neighborhood. It wasn't an unfriendly visit, really. He normally extracted a small tax, some food that was left unattended. Tonight he smelled food in one of the backpacks. With sharp teeth and slashing claws the toll collector gathered his dues. When the family awoke the backpack was in shreds. The contents were scattered over a wide area.

The third day the family left the protection of the forest and began to climb. As far as the dad remembered, this mountain wasn't on the map. It was an arduous climb. Legs burned. Backs ached. Backpack chafed. Wind mixed with sleet lashed their faces. Ice covered the rock making the ascent dangerous. In the late afternoon the mother slipped. She broke her leg just above the ankle.

To make matters worse, all four hikers were coming to the growing realization that they were lost. The brother took on the role of the joker in order to lighten the tension. The mother was in pain and now the pain was blended with deep worry. The father was serious, very concerned about how he was going to extract his family from this mounting crisis. The sister was downright angry. She was angry with her brother for acting dumb in such a situation, angry with her mother for falling, and angry with her father for getting them into all of this.

By nightfall the father admitted what they all knew. They were lost. Originally they had food supplies for four days. However, the bear raid had robbed them of important stores. One of their water jugs had also been punctured.

Dinner was meager. The ground seemed harder. The mother was extremely uncomfortable. The laughter was gone.

The fourth day was a chore. They worked up a sweat and as soon as it trickled down their backs it seemed to freeze. They grew tired quickly. Father and son alternated providing support for the mother. The ground was icy and therefore treacherous. They slid and stumbled all day long searching in vain for a trail out of this wilderness. Nothing. And to think, this was to have been the night they were to have slept in their own beds.

The fifth and sixth days were more of the same. The camera was now packed away. They weren't in the mood to take pictures anyway. The family members silently focused on survival.

On the afternoon of day six the weary travelers sheltered in some pines. Family morale was at an all-time low. Off in the distance the mother saw movement; then again she thought it might be something flashing. The fading light of day was shining off of something, of that she was sure. What it was, not one of the four could imagine. Although extremely tired they went to investigate. Strange. It was a mirror. "Who in their right mind would place a mirror in the middle of this wilderness?" they thought.

Had they taken the time, they would have been able to see a reflection of the pine forest around them. They were much too exhausted to even care about such things. What they clearly saw in the mirror was a reflection of their true condition. They were disheveled. Their faces were dirt-streaked. They looked hungry. The men needed to shave. The ladies' hair stuck out at odd angles from beneath their stocking hats. Their clothes were torn and soiled. They were broken in spirit and body. They decided that all this present suffering was the result of bad choices. With emotions barely in check, the dad apologized again for getting them into this situation.

In spite of themselves they pulled out the camera and snapped a picture beside the mirror. The picture revealed not only the family's physical distress, but if you looked into the eyes of those photographed, you could see deep dissatisfaction and desperate despair. No smiles. No sense of expectation. No real hope. They were lost and that was it.

The snow that had been lightly falling all day was beginning to pile up. They knew they would have to spend another night in the cold. They shivered involuntarily. They would try to hunker down out of the wind and make the best of a worsening situation. Food supplies were almost gone. They had been on a bare-bones ration for the past two days.

They camped that night near the mirror. It provided them a small degree of comfort. Maybe it was because someone had planted that mirror in this wilderness, in their wilderness. Someone had actually been where they were. In a crazy kind of logic the father was comforted by thinking, "If someone has been here to plant this mirror, then in some way at least that one can understand our situation."

The next morning they wanted very much to stay in their sleeping bags. Yet, they knew they needed to get up. The daughter had a strange feeling. It was like her depression and anger were lifting. She went to the mirror. Again she looked in. She saw the same bedraggled face. She saw eyes that were lifeless, globs of sleep attached to the corners. She saw hair, a mop really. She saw … wait … in the distance, she couldn't believe what she saw. She saw a green Volkswagen van. An explosion of joy erupted from her soul. "The car! I see the car! We are safe!"

On the drive home in the warm van each reflected back on their journey. Mostly it was done in silence. "I can't believe we spent an extra night in those pines," Father said. "How come we weren't able to see the van in the mirror last night?" A few suggestions were given. Everyone agreed it was the mother who came up with the most realistic answer. "We were so lost, so disoriented, so cold, so tired, so consumed with our situation, that we couldn't even see the van."

Just before climbing in the van for the ride home, the family stopped to take the last picture on the roll. Happy faces replaced sad ones. Oh, they were still dirty, but the eyes bespoke relief and joy. They had been saved and they knew it.

Postscript

*I*t seemed fitting to me, somehow, to conclude this collection of stories and essays with another story. The story "Rescued Through the Mirror," although a "stretch" as some might say, is an attempt to recap the entire message of Genesis chapters one through eleven in an allegory of sorts. In this allegory every piece of the narrative should not be pressed for meaning but, all in all, it says something like this:

At the beginning of the trail the family was clean, equipped, and eager. The camera recorded their condition. They had a map that offered not only direction but also warning. They chose to disregard both. This rebellion brought about their downfall. While in search of adventure they encountered many troubles. Nature that was once gracious and welcoming literally turned the cold shoulder to them. Mistaken directions and missteps plunged them into a life-threatening situation. By the time they found their way back to the "sheltering pines" they were very near home but they didn't know it. Near those pines they came upon the mirror. In that mirror they were able to discover their true state: helpless, restless, lost, broken, hungry, dirty, and defeated. Again, the camera was used to record their condition. It was in the mirror that the sister saw what she had really become and, at the same time, saw the van that would take them home. The last exposure on the roll of film recorded their relief. In spite of their waywardness, they were going to be safe.

Genesis chapters one through eleven is like a mirror planted by God in the wilderness. It reveals our self-inflicted condition in a no-holds-barred fashion. It reveals a perfect world turned cold, almost antagonistic against us. The stories tell us we have caused creation to work against us. These stories also reveal a God who searches for, longs for, and works for our rescue.

Of course, the whole story of God's saving action is not found in Genesis alone. The map in the story is a simple picture of God's

Word. One of the hardest things for me was to share these Genesis
stories without reference to the cross of Jesus Christ. If you read
closely you can see that the finished work of Jesus was not far from
my mind as I wrote.

I believe that we need these stories of the beginning. They are
foundational for our lives of faith. In the first eleven chapters of
Genesis we learn of God's marvelous provision and the high regard
that he has for us. We see our self-imposed circumstances and the
devastating consequences of our sinfulness. But, if we are not careful,
we can focus our attention so much on our sorry state, the fallen
mess that we have created of our lives, that we miss the extended
grace and glorious provision of God. It must be realized that these
early stories of Genesis are not complete in themselves. They are
only a reflection, a prelude, if you will, to God's completed story, the
in-breaking story. This is the truthful narrative of Jesus: God became
man, the very one who lived and died on the cross and rose again.
All of this was done in search of, and for the redemption and rescue
of his most prized creations, you and me.

In I Peter we find this summary: "You were rescued from the
useless life that you learned from your ancestors. But you know that
you were not rescued by such things as silver and gold that don't last
forever. You were rescued by the precious blood of Christ, that
spotless and innocent lamb. Christ was chosen even before the world
was created, but because of you, he didn't come until these last days"
(1:18-20, C.E.V.).